MOVING
TO
TAMPA
THE UN-TOURIST GUIDE

MARY LOU JANSON

CONTENTS

FOREWORD

WHY I LIVE IN TAMPA
BY RICHARD GONZMART

Tampa is my home and I can't imagine living anywhere else.

Why would I?

I found my life's love here. I found my life's work here. I found lifelong friends here.

My ancestors came to Tampa's Ybor City in 1902, and this city has allowed us to live the American dream. My great-grandfather Casimio Hernandez, Sr. – a Cuban immigrant -- started the Columbia Restaurant in 1905. It's still owned by our family and is now the oldest restaurant in Florida and the largest Spanish restaurant in the world.

In addition to studying restaurants and hospitality in Denver and Madrid, and running one of our restaurants in St. Augustine, I've been fortunate enough to travel all over the U.S. and the world: Europe, Asia, South America, the Caribbean and Africa.

I'm glad to go, but I'm even happier when I return to Tampa.

It's not just the average temperature of 72 degrees or the more than 1,300 miles of beaches.

This area has world-class airport and arts venues in Tampa International Airport and the David A. Straz, Jr. Center for the Performing Arts. We have NFL, NHL and MLB teams with the Buccaneers, Lightning and Rays. The Bucs won a Super Bowl, the Lightning won the Stanley Cup and the Rays played in the World Series.

We've hosted four Super Bowls, one NCAA Final Four, one NCAA Frozen Four, Men's and Women's Soccer Championships and the 2017 NCAA College Football Championship is next.

We have one of the top medical research facilities in the country at Moffitt Cancer Center, where I am convinced they will find a cure for cancer.

We have wonderful educational facilities in the University of South Florida, Hillsborough Community College and the University of Tampa. I spent my high school years at Jesuit, where I learned the meaning of discipline and integrity. And I learned that through hard work and commitment, anything is possible.

That's especially true in Tampa. This is an area of immigrants – from the Native Americans to European explorers to the Cuban cigar workers and on and on until today when people still arrive seeking opportunity and a better life.

Tampa has history and new beginnings, founding families and energetic newcomers, tradition and new ideas.

We sometimes like to say that Tampa itself is like paella – composed of many different ingredients that together provide its unique flavor. Sometimes we say it's like a Cuban sandwich or "a mixto," as they used to call it, because of how each nationality settling in Tampa brought its own flavors to the popular sandwich.

But no matter where you come from, if you're willing to work hard and commit, it's possible to enjoy great personal and professional success in Tampa.

I think about my great-grandfather, who came to America from Cuba hoping for a new start and new freedoms. He loved his new home country so much that he named the restaurant for a patriotic song, "Columbia, Gem of the Ocean," which once was being considered to become the U.S. National Anthem.

Charitable to the core, he offered three daily meals to workers for five dollars a month.

"It is democratic in the extreme," a newspaper reporter wrote of the Columbia at the time. "If a working man wants a Cuban sandwich and a glass of Tropical Ale, he enters the corner door, dressed however he may be, and sits down to one. All day long, workers sit around as if at home."

There were many hard years between then and now, including those during the Depression, Prohibition, World Wars and urban renewal.

But through four and now five generations, we have held down our corner of Ybor City, expanded to 1,700 seats and 15 dining rooms, and even opened six other Florida locations including two Columbia Cafés in Tampa.

And now we're opening a new concept, Ulele, which is named for a legendary Indian princess. The site is the 1903 former Water Works plant near downtown Tampa, with cool river breezes and gorgeous sunsets.

The restaurant and on-site brewery will serve unique foods and spirits by fusing elements from a rich variety of Native American and multicultural influences, including those of European explorers. The menu will feature items indigenous to this area's waters and farms. The food will be local and fresh, naturally.

The on-site brewery will create craft-made beers. The wine list will exclusively feature domestic wines from family-owned vineyards all across the U.S. We'll also create Ulele signature cocktails.

Like Tampa, we celebrate the past and look to the future. This is a great place to work and play.

Why would I live anywhere else?

RICHARD GONZMART is the fourth generation owner operator of the Columbia Restaurant Group, founded in 1905 in Tampa's Ybor City.

The Columbia has won hundreds of awards, including:

Named an All-American Icon by Nation's Restaurant News, one of only 50 restaurants in the U.S. chosen for this honor in 2010.

- Earned the "Distinguished Restaurants of North America (DiRoNA) Award of Excellence" every year from 2005 to the present. One of the most prestigious awards in the fine dining industry.
- Named to Nation's Restaurant News Fine Dining Hall of Fame.

INTRODUCTION
TAMPA - NATURALLY APPEALING, INCREDIBLY INVITING

Native American Indians, Spanish explorers and swashbuckling pirates were the first to discover the special charms of this city by the bay. What was a sparsely populated area primarily inhabited by palmettos, pines and scrubs, gradually grew from a modest port town into a major metropolitan area that still manages to exude the warmth and welcoming feel of a much smaller city.

Its waterfront, a landscape filled with lush, tropical foliage and the year-round sunshine and warm weather so typical of Florida, define the area's natural beauty.

Not just another pretty place, Tampa is a vibrant city boasting and hosting a world class, international airport, professional sports teams, high-end retail, fine dining experiences, multi-national companies, state-of-the-art medical facilities, colleges and universities, MacDill Air Force Base and so much more.

That's not to say it's all work and no play around these parts. Tampa knows how to throw a party, whether hosting a Super Bowl, welcoming the 2012 Republican National Convention or rolling out the red carpet for the International Indian Film Academy's so-called Bollywood Oscars awarded here in April 2014.

This Central Florida West Coast community is also an ideal place to start a career, start a family or start enjoying retirement. From the lofts located in Ybor City to the bungalows of Seminole Heights, and from the high-rise luxury condominiums lining Bayshore Boulevard to the gated communities of New Tampa, there are living spaces for all lifestyles.

Tampa also offers plenty of perks such as parks and playgrounds, museums and arts districts, golf courses and tennis courts, opera and orchestras and aquariums and zoos. Everything you need for a well-rounded lifestyle is available and easily accessible no matter where you reside in the Tampa area.

One of the most compelling reasons to make Tampa your new home is best summed up by Rick Homans, president and CEO of the Tampa Hillsborough Economic Development Corp.:

"Currently, the Tampa metropolitan area leads the state of Florida in job gains. In the past two years alone, more than 50 companies have selected Hillsborough County as the site of their relocation and expansion activities, generating over 8,700 new jobs and $688 million in capital investment. Global market leaders, including Bristol-Myers Squibb, Morgan Stanley, The Depository Trust & Clearing Corporation, Time Warner Business Services, USAA and Amazon have expressed their confidence in our community by announcing plans for significant, strategic growth."

Whatever your reason for moving here, you'll find our book a compelling guide chock full of insights and information to make you feel right at home.

Downtown Tampa skyline at night

A Few Fun Facts

For newcomers, former residents who may be returning to their roots or anyone who needs to get quickly up to speed about Tampa, there are a few things you need to know.

- You are not living in Tampa Bay. That term is loosely used by news crews and sportscasters who don't understand that it is a regional reference and not a specific city.

- Native or newcomer, while living in Tampa, you are likely to be referred to as either a Tampanian or a Tampan.

- Nicknames for your new hometown include Cigar City, The Big Guava, Lightning Capital of the World and Cigar Capital of the World. Tampa was known worldwide for its hand-rolled cigars.

- Native American Indians are believed to have named this area Tanpa, a word thought to mean "Sticks of Fire," inspired by its frequent lightning storms.

- And Big Guava? Steve Otto, a Tampa Tribune newspaper columnist, insisted if New York could be the Big Apple it was only right Tampa's claim to fame should be guavas.

- Every year the city is invaded by hundreds of pirates, in elaborate costume and make-up, who arrive aboard a fully rigged pirate ship, not in search of treasure but simply for pleasure. Gasparilla has been a Tampa tradition since the early 1900s and locals plan pirate-themed parties that stretch from early morning until late night. Eye patches and talking like a pirate, that day in particular, are encouraged.

Ten Reasons to Live in Tampa (In No Particular Order)

1. **Natural Beauty.** Lush foliage, sparkling waterfronts and nightly displays of colorful sunsets are just part of the allure of this West Coast community. Tall palm trees add a tropical touch, bays, lakes, rivers and other bodies of water are in abundance and a year 'round growing season means something's always in bloom.

Beautiful views abound throughout the Tampa area

2. **Wonderful Weather.** This Central Florida, west coast community typically boasts temperatures and clear skies that make it possible to enjoy outdoor activities year-round. That means playing golf and tennis, going fishing and boating or enjoying cycling and running with only a slight seasonal adjustment of outdoor attire.

3. **Excellent Entertainment.** The range of world-class performers who make appearances here throughout the year is an impressive list that includes top opera singers to rock stars, touring productions of hit Broadway shows to professional

dance companies and classical musicians to kings and queens of comedy.

Historic Tampa Theatre is one of the many venues that bring world class entertainment to the city

4. **Casual Lifestyle.** Although black tie galas and lots of elegant events frequently crowd social calendars, for the most part, the day-to-day dress code is more relaxed than restrained. The look can be tropical cool, neatly chic or very vintage but the key is dressing for comfort and climate.

5. **Spectacular Sports.** Fans have a lot to cheer about whether it is for professional sports like NFL Football's the Tampa Bay Buccaneers, Major League Baseball's the Tampa Bay Rays, the National Hockey League's Tampa Bay Lightning, spring training when the New York Yankees are on deck at Steinbrenner Field or the North American Soccer League's Tampa Bay Rowdies. Annual sports events include two leading teams competing in college football's Outback Bowl and the high-speed action of the Firestone Grand Prix IndyCar series race across the streets of St. Petersburg.

6. **Great Outdoors.** Tampa offers everything from private golf courses to public parks, offshore to deep-sea fishing, canoe

and kayak excursions to stand up paddle boarding, hiking and biking to running and sunning.

Sunrise to sunset enjoy year round recreational activities in Tampa

7. **Wild to Mild.** Our city boasts many great ways to observe all sorts of native to non-native creatures. We are a top bird migratory and watching spot as well as a great place to be entertained by manatees and dolphins moving along the waterfront. Major attractions like Busch Gardens Tampa Bay, Lowry Park Zoo and the Florida Aquarium deliver all sorts of wildlife encounters while Big Cat Rescue serves as a sanctuary for rescued, rehabilitating and endangered species of big cats.

8. **Multi-cultural, multi-ethnic.** Tampa is a melting pot that welcomes people from around the world and all sorts of cultural influences. This rich diversity is recognized during annual festivals, special events and parades and featured at ethnic restaurants. Tampa is also is the home to the nation's only tri-lingual newspaper, La Gaceta, which is published in English, Spanish and Italian.

9. **Great Gateway.** With its world-class airport, lively cruise ship terminal, cross-country AMTRAK railroad service and major interstate highway connections, Tampa is perfect for

locals who travel for work or for pleasure. Whether traveling by air, water or land, these connectors make it easy to go anywhere in the world.

Tampa Union Station welcomes train passengers traveling on AMTRAK

10. **Urban to Suburban.** Looking for a loft in the city center or longing for a piece of land where you can plant a garden? Want to restore a bungalow back to its original beauty or need a deluxe home complete with its own dock? Then Tampa's got a spot for you. Select from historic neighborhoods to condos overlooking the Port of Tampa. Opt for a waterfront view from a colonial-style Bayshore mansion or go for the gusto of living adjacent to a private golf course.

CHAPTER 1
BACKGROUND CHECK

Brief History of Tampa

Tampa's transformation from a small, swampy, barely-there village to a major, multi-cultural metropolis owes a great deal to a colorful cast of characters who helped shape this city's fortunes and future.

First to call this Central Florida West Coast area home were Native American Indians likely drawn by the abundance of game, a semi-tropical climate, fertile soil and a waterfront brimming with fish. It is believed Caloosa Indians dubbed the village they inhabited Tanpa, a word meaning "sticks of fire," possibly inspired by the dramatic lightning displays that light up the sky. However, when the name was recorded, it was officially written as Tampa.

European explorers later followed, making their way into Tampa Bay, coming ashore and trekking into the Florida wilderness, many driven by a desire to find gold while others began life in a new land.

Eventually other settlers followed as Tampa transitioned into an area teeming with troops, traders and pioneers drawn by the area's lively port and military fort. It officially became a U.S. territory in 1845.

By the late 1800s, a railroad baron named Henry B. Plant greatly impacted the area's growth when he extended his rail system here, creating a vital link for travelers and trade. Over the next few years, the city's population reportedly exploded from several hundred to more than 3,000.

A bridge across the Hillsborough River proved to be key not only to connecting the downtown district with the rest of the city but also to prompting Plant to build a lavish resort on the west banks of the river. The Tampa Bay Hotel opened to great fanfare in 1891, welcoming visitors who flocked here to enjoy Florida's warm, winter weather as well as celebrities, athletes and politicians who graced its grounds over the years. The original building still stands with its signature silver minarets creating a striking silhouette against the downtown skyline. No longer a hotel, the building is now home to the University of Tampa.

The former Tampa Bay Hotel is now the University of Tampa

Meanwhile, just east of downtown, Vicente Martinez Ybor was purchasing land and building the first of many factories that produced hand-rolled cigars. The industry would eventually employ nearly 12,000 workers and bring what became known as Ybor City global fame as the "Cigar Capital of the World."

When the combined impact of mechanization, the rising popularity of cigarettes and the Depression decimated the labor-intensive industry, many of the immigrants who worked in the factories found new livelihoods and stayed. Generations later, their descendants continue to enrich the diversity and cultural heritage that is a vital characteristic of this area.

Ybor City is a designated National Historic Landmark District

Waterways have always played a role in Tampa's past, from the time pirates plied its coast until shiploads of phosphate set sail from its docks. Port Tampa continues to fuel economic development as cargo ships and passenger cruise lines continuously drop anchor at its terminals, generating enough activity and revenue to rank this among the nation's largest ports.

Aviation has also been critical to boosting Tampa's profile for commerce and travel, both nationally as well as internationally. Tampa Bay's milestone contribution to aviation history dates back to 1914, when the world's first scheduled commercial airline service was successfully launched by the St. Petersburg-Tampa Airboat Line and piloted by Tony Jannus.

No history of Tampa would be complete without mention of its military presence and personnel. When the U.S. declared war on Spain in 1898, Tampa was the port of embarkation for troops headed to Cuba. And it was here that a colorful colonel named Theodore (Teddy) Roosevelt organized the first volunteer cavalry in the Spanish-American War, the "Rough Riders."

Because of its strategic location during that war, Tampa was selected as the site where troops gathered before shipping off for Cuba. A camp established to accommodate the thousands of personnel amassed here was located in what was then known as Port Tampa City. That former encampment now borders what has become a major military installation, MacDill Air Force Base.

MacDill Air Force Base, an active U.S. Air Force base, was officially activated in 1941

MacDill Air Force Base, perched on the southwestern tip of Tampa, is also headquarters for U.S. Central Command (USCENTCOM) and U.S. Special Operations Command (USSOCOM).

Today, Tampa is far from a fishing village. The city and its surrounding communities represent a diverse mix of industries that include agriculture, tourism, technology, health care, financial services and transportation.

Tampa remains an area of growth and opportunity and retains many of the original features that first attracted inhabitants to its shore.

Tampa Facts at a Glance

- Largest city in Hillsborough County and the county seat
- Third most populous city in Florida.
- About one-third of the population of Hillsborough County lives in Tampa
- Economic base includes tourism, agriculture, construction, finance, health care, government, technology and Port of Tampa.

Source: City of Tampa (www.tampagov.net/about_us)

Tampa Bay

- Metropolitan area comprised of Tampa-St. Petersburg-Clearwater

- Four-county area is composed of nearly 2.9 million residents

- Ranks as second largest metropolitan statistical area (MS) in Florida and fourth largest in the Southeastern U.S.

Source: Wikipedia: www.en.wikipedia.org/wiki/Tampa,_Florida

City of Tampa mural located in the downtown Tampa business district

CHAPTER 2

GEOGRAPHIC AND COMMUNITY GUIDE TO TAMPA

Located midway along Central Florida's West Coast, Tampa's central location is primarily a low-lying and plateau-like area, similar to much of the state's landscape. The predominantly sea level city is bordered by Old Tampa Bay and Hillsborough Bay, large bodies of water that unite to form Tampa Bay which feeds into the Gulf of Mexico.

The Hillsborough River is the primary source of freshwater for this area. It flows from the north before passing through downtown Tampa and eventually emptying into Hillsborough Bay.

Getting to Know Hillsborough Communities

Tampa is the largest of three incorporated cities in Hillsborough County as well as the county seat.

Spanning 1,020 square miles of land and 24 miles of inland water area, Hillsborough ranked as Florida's fourth most populated county in 2012, tallying an estimated 1.28 million people, according to the U.S. Census Bureau.

Tampa's population equaled 347,645 in 2012, with the remaining two incorporated areas, Plant City and Temple Terrace, contributing an additional 35,903 and 25,189 residents, respectively.

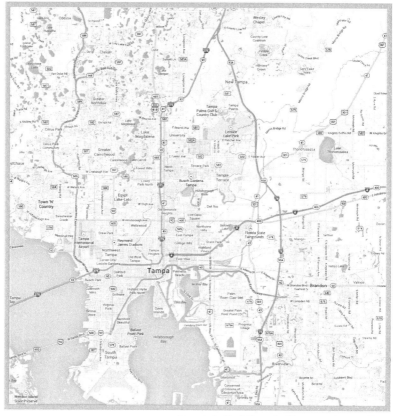

See detailed Google Map version online:
www.google.com/maps/@28.0247907,-82.4686195,11z

Government offices and professional firms fill downtown Tampa and the Westshore area boasts the highest concentration of office space (4,000 businesses and more than 93,000 employees) in Florida. But, both areas boast growing residential bases and throughout Tampa there are multiple housing options, ranging from quiet neighborhoods to industrial-looking lofts.

Among the oldest neighborhoods are Hyde Park and Seminole Heights, formerly forlorn areas that have been, or are being, lovingly restored, revitalized and reinvigorated and now boast award-winning architecture and well maintained lawns.

Residents, who want to be close to the water as well as to downtown Tampa, can become island-dwellers by living on either Harbour Island or Davis Islands.

An aerial view of Davis Islands and the downtown Tampa waterfront

Harbour Island is a more recent mixed-used development dominated by luxury homes, high-rise offices and a high-end hotel.

Just across the channel is Davis Islands, a collection of islands with homes ranging from modest to mansions, as well as Peter O'Knight Airport, primarily used for private planes and flight instruction, and one of the area's leading medical facilities, Tampa General Hospital.

Areas like Ybor City and West Tampa remain vital links to Tampa's past. They have been predominantly influenced by Hispanic, Cuban, and Italian populations for generations and are distinguished by red brick streets and former cigar factories refurbished into offices and artists' studios.

Some of the city's most stately homes are nestled along the tree-lined, scenic streets of Ballast Point, Palma Ceia, and the waterfront bordered by Bayshore Boulevard. Many of the city's prominent politicians and business leaders have either grown up or raised families of their own here.

One of the newer and more noticeable residential areas, with its concentration of high rise residential towers, is the Channel District that offers views of Tampa's working port and the downtown skyline.

The Channel District features towers of condos and apartment in an urban setting

Because most of the city's most central areas are already heavily populated and densely developed, growth has been forced to spread to the north and east. Areas where there once were more farms than families and citrus groves than grocery stores are now filled with single-family homes, retail centers and multi-lane thoroughfares.

Ever-expanding unincorporated areas like Carrollwood remain popular spots for families and businesses. Likewise, eastward to Brandon, vibrant commercial and residential development continues while new subdivisions in Westchase, Tampa Palms and New Tampa help accommodate the area's on-going growth as more and more people are attracted by the affordability and affability of these areas.

Why Tampa Bay?

People choose places to live for many different reasons, but for me, the airport in Tampa was quite an important factor when I moved here from England 24 years ago. For anyone who travels, the airport is very well planned, and it's usually possible to be driving out in a car within 15 minutes of landing. Because it's close to the city, the airport is also only 15-20 minutes from some of the best residential areas in Tampa Bay.

Madeleine Krasne

The lifestyle choices offered here are abundant. There are high-end condominiums and large mansions lining Bayshore Boulevard offering million-dollar views of the waterfront that are also close to the downtown business district and the many amenities of South Tampa.

There are great restaurants, good sports facilities and, of course, the proximity to water is great for boat lovers. The Tampa Bay area has waterfront homes with open bay views and, on the west side of the peninsula, there are canals with easy access to the bay. Marinas and membership-based yacht clubs are conveniently located on Davis Islands, Harbour Island and in the Ballast Point area of South Tampa so if your home does not include private docking facilities, you can still enjoy find a nearby spot for your sailboat, powerboat or yacht.

For those who prefer a gated community near downtown, Harbour Island offers security, a manicured landscape, waterfront homes, plus the convenience of Harbour Island Athletic Club, which has tennis courts, an outdoor pool and extensive gym facilities.

The local weather is one of the major influences for anyone who enjoys outdoor activities. The warm, sunny, clear days of our winters, coupled with an average daytime temperature around 70 degrees, makes it possible to enjoy the outdoors for most of the year. Activities such as sailing, paddle-boarding and canoeing are all available in many places. South Tampa boasts two yacht clubs, the Tampa Yacht Club and the Davis Island Yacht Club, both of which have an active membership and social facilities.

It's not all about the water, either. For golf lovers, there are excellent tournament courses plus several golf resorts in the vicinity, some offering high-end homes around the perimeter. The northern areas of the city, like Avila, Hunter's Green and Tampa Palms, also offer some beautiful gated communities with larger homes and large lots, for those wanting acreage and more privacy.

For families, school districts are important, and those with young children favor the shaded, tree-lined streets of South Tampa's Hyde Park historic district. Old Hyde Park Village provides a pleasant stroll around its smaller shops and restaurants and is also a great location for art festivals, Sunday markets and outdoor jazz nights. In terms of amenities, the arts are not forgotten, with a major focus being the downtown area.

The Performing Arts Center (known as the Straz Center) contains several theaters and houses major musical productions, plays and some fringe activities. The Tampa Museum of Art is close by, and is constantly changing its offerings. The downtown area is enhanced by the Hillsborough River, which forms its western border, another pleasant feature of the city.

The homes in Tampa Bay are also quite varied in style. In many cases, older, single-story homes have been replaced by modern, elevated homes, often with Mediterranean styling, although some custom homes are very individual.

There's also the pleasant community of Davis Islands with its wide streets and eclectic atmosphere, which is where I live. Charming and quirky are some of the adjectives that describe what once was a pile of silt and is now home to around 5,000 people. The short stretch of East Davis Boulevard has the feel of a busy, small village center. It's close to major highways, convenient for getting around, surrounded by water and naturally beautiful, ideal for biking, walking or running and perfect for walks with my Labrador.

And it has one of the few real beaches in Tampa, which makes this ideal for water-oriented sports like paddle-boarding.

The weather also allows semi-tropical landscaping, so that palm trees and large flowering vegetation such as hibiscus and bougainvillea add a relaxed beauty to the environment.

So whatever is most important to you, it's highly likely that this city can offer a rewarding place to live. Come and see!

MADELEINE KRASNE CLHMS
Broker Associate
Premier Sotheby's International Reality
www.sothebysrealty.com

Getting Around Town

What is commonly referred to as the Tampa Bay area is comprised of Tampa, St. Petersburg and Clearwater and boasts a combined population base representing some 2.9 million residents.

Residents of both Hillsborough and Pinellas counties commonly commute between both areas, with students, professionals and part-time workers opting to live on one side of Tampa Bay while attending college or finding employment on the opposite side of the bay.

Beautiful waterfront views are one of this area's many natural amenities but those are limited to bays, lakes and rivers. A direct view of the

Gulf of Mexico requires a drive over to neighboring Pinellas County, home of both St. Petersburg and Clearwater.

Tampa is a city that primarily requires a vehicle for ease, quickness and comfort of getting around. Taxis and buses are options but our community is so spread out that those can quickly become pricey and time-consuming.

The area's leading high-speed, heavy volume roadways are I-275 and I-75 that serve as the major north-south thoroughfares. Both connect with I-4 which is a heavily used highway continuing through Orlando to Florida's east coast.

Residents can easily access the waterfront from areas throughout Tampa

Without any major mass transportation options in the near future, traffic and parking are issues just about anywhere in the city and at any time of day or night.

Only downtown Tampa offers an option of riding either the rubber-tired In-Town Trolley or electric TECO Line Streetcar that moves multiple passengers around within a limited area for a fee.

Electric vehicle charging stations are slowly spreading throughout the city offering those with a plug-in vehicle an option to park and charge for a fee.

Sources: Tampa By the Numbers

www.quickfacts.census.gov/qfd/index.html

www.city-data.com/city/Tampa-Florida.html

TECO Line Streetcar connects Ybor City and the Channel District with downtown Tampa

The Climate

Fortunately waterways tend to offer some relief from Florida heat. Bay breezes deliver a cooling touch that makes summertime highs hovering near, or into, the 90s a bit more bearable. Tampa's temperate, semi-tropical climate does not necessarily end with the onset of fall or even winter. Warm weather tends to linger here long after it has abandoned other areas of the country.

When temperatures do eventually drop, the contrast creates a welcome briskness and adds a slight brace to the air.

The area's normally placid waterfronts can become turbulent during tropical storms and hurricanes. Waterspouts have become increasingly common during summer months, creating dramatic glimpses of tall, dark spirals that can be a real distraction to drivers crossing bridges and a danger to nearby boaters. When sufficient rain coincides with high tides, that combination can create flood conditions that may make some roads un-passable or even result in mandatory evacuations.

Heat and humidity are noticeable throughout much of the year while winters tend to be a bit more mild and marked by drier conditions. Occasional freezes have been recorded but winter temperatures typically hover around the 50-degree mark.

Hurricane season is generally defined as June through November but sometimes Mother Nature makes her own timeline. Historically there have been severe hurricanes that have created widespread devastation but nothing of that magnitude has hit the Tampa Bay area lately. There have been no major hurricanes or direct hits here since 1921 but there have been plenty of major storms and close calls. The most recent rash of hard-hitting weather was in 2004. The 2013 Atlantic hurricane season was the least harrowing in 30 years.

Still, hurricanes are a fact of life and preparation can be key to survival. Residents are accustomed to going through a hurricane preparedness checklist every year and an increasing number of households now have generators in case electric power is lost for long periods of time.

Basics may include knowing where to move your car to higher ground if you live in a flood prone area. If you have a four-legged friend, stock up on pet food as well as people food and have an evacuation destination in mind that welcomes pets. Make sure medical supplies and first aid kits are well stocked and prescriptions are current.

Be sure to know your evacuation routes and shelter locations in advance.

Because power failures may kill your ATM and close your gas station, keep a supply of cash handy all season long and don't leave filling your car's gas tank until the last minute.

Hillsborough County officials recommend having enough supplies on hand to last at least three days. That includes food that does not require cooking or refrigeration, plenty of water for drinking and flashlights with extra batteries.

Most important, mandatory evacuations need to be heeded. While hurricanes are unpredictable it is always important to remember to protect yourself and loved ones. Homes and businesses can be repaired or replaced.

CHAPTER 3
CHOOSING WHERE TO LIVE IN TAMPA

Tampa is literally a city for all ages and all phases of life. The housing mix ranges from apartment buildings to town homes, single-family bungalows to urban lofts and grand mansions to luxury penthouses.

Whether beginning a career or enjoying your retirement, there are areas that may be more suited to your lifestyle and more appropriate for your particular interests than others.

SoHo, a residential and commercial area named for its South Howard location, is well known for pub crawls, happy hour specials and nightlife while Sun City Center, which is found south of Tampa, is an age-restricted community where active seniors live and are known to commute short distances by golf cart.

Tampa is, above all, a welcoming community that strives to be a good neighbor to all. Families, retirees, young professionals and same sex couples can be found living, working and enjoying leisure time activities throughout the city and its surrounding communities.

While dwelling on just where to find your dwelling, keep in mind that options are plentiful. Want to be immersed in an urban setting, prefer a more "green" vantage point from a home overlooking a manicured golf course, love to be surrounded by history or want to cast your gaze on the sparkling waterfront and bustling Port Tampa Bay? Then you're in the right place.

Cost of Housing

Here are some representative prices of various sizes and styles of housing in the Tampa, Florida area.

$379,900 - Downtown Tampa: 2 BR/2 B 8th floor 1152 sq. ft. condo
$1.29M - Hyde Park: 5BR/4B 4262 sq. ft. single family
$300,000 - New Tampa: 4BR/3B 2688 sq. ft. single family
$849,000 - Culbreath Isles: 3BR/3B 2200 sq. ft. canal front single family
$375,000 - Seminole Heights: Classic 1924 4BR/2B 2501 sq. ft. home
$300,000 - Apollo Beach: 3BR/2B 2104 sq. ft. waterfront ranch
$264,900 - Westchase: 3BR/3B $2315 sq. ft. townhome
$199,000 - Carrollwood Village—3BR/3B 1685 sq. ft. single family
Source: Zillow.com

Happily, most neighborhoods in the Tampa area provide a broad range of housing options from very affordable to very expensive. Thus, you are likely to find just the right home in a wide range of neighborhoods.

Compare Tampa options to what you can buy around the country:

- $550,000 - A one-bedroom condo in downtown Boston

- $700,000 - A 1940s two-bedroom home in Los Angeles

- $800,000 - Roughly five acres of land to build a home in Far Hills, New Jersey

- $1 million - A three-bedroom home in Washington, D.C that dates back to the eighteen hundreds

- $400,000 – A newly constructed town home in Houston, Texas

- $300,000 – A two-bedroom condo in downtown Minneapolis

- $650,000 – A one-bedroom, one-bath condo in Long Island, New York

Know Your Tampa Neighborhoods

Here is a breakdown of some of the signature Tampa neighborhoods and a gauge of what types of rental rates and sales prices you could encounter.

For a snapshot of what areas are hot and what prices those listings are generating. check out the Tampa Real Estate Overview on Trulia. Here is an example of the information it provides:

"The average listing price for homes for sale in Tampa FL was $261,000 for the week ending Feb 26, which represents a decrease of 1.8%, or $4,916, compared to the prior week. Popular neighborhoods in Tampa include Old Seminole Heights and Tampa Palms, with average listing prices of $131,905 and $361,308."

A comprehensive overview of the average listing price sales price and price per square foot can be found on Trulia's Tampa Home Prices page.

Rental rates for homes and apartments vary widely based on location, square footage and amenities. For insights into the area's inventory and price points for housing rentals, check out Tampa Houses for Rent on Zillow.com. And visit Zillow.com for Tampa Apartment Rentals information.

Downtown Tampa offers an increasingly vibrant mix of apartments and condos, rentals and sales. This area is perfect for people who work downtown and love the idea of walking to their workplace or those who are patrons of the arts or sports fans and are happy to stroll to the performing arts center, hockey arena or whatever concert, festival or special event is happening downtown. There are select retail establishments nearby. Duckweed Urban Market, billed as Downtown Tampa's Neighborhood Grocery Store, features ready-to-eat meals, craft beers, pet food and basics like locally roasted ground coffees and freshly baked goods.

Duckweed Urban Market is the neighborhood grocery for Tampa's downtown.

Historic neighborhoods like Hyde Park, east of downtown, and Seminole Heights, centrally located just north of the downtown district, are considered desirable places to live for their looks and lifestyle. Tree-lined streets, front porches, well-cared-for lawns and tastefully restored or renovated homes -- from elegant Southern Colonial architecture to quaint Craftsman-style bungalows - are the norm for these highly residential areas. Both areas have undergone resurgences but Hyde Park is considered to be the more polished and prestigious address while Seminole Heights is viewed as a more eclectic, artsy area in terms of its residents and aesthetic.

Harbour Island and Davis Islands are large land masses that were created by dredging. Both boast an abundance of waterfront, offer rentals as well as condominiums and single-family residences and provide residents with convenient locations to the downtown area as well as easy access to major east-west and north-south connectors. Harbour Island had little more than a phosphate terminal on its land until the 80s when a developer added commercial ventures like office space, a hotel and restaurants. Residential development now dominates the island and prices are at a premium. Davis Islands offers quite a range of possibilities from stately homes to historical buildings that offer apartments, to modest duplexes, from traditional to contemporary single-family homes and even a mansion owned by New York Yankees professional baseball player Derek Jeter.

Originally developed in the 1960s, Culbreath Isles was one of the first gated, waterfront communities established in Tampa. It remains one of the few private enclaves of its kind in South Tampa. Lovely homes have gradually been supplanted by ever more luxurious mansions that propel prices to the million-dollar-plus level. This area is a real draw for those who like to dock their yachts and sailboats close to home. Residents are within minutes of Tampa International Airport, are conveniently close to upscale dining and shopping and are considered to live in one of the area's most desirable school districts.

An established Tampa neighborhood that dates back to the late 1800s, Carrollwood was flush with citrus groves and cattle ranches for decades. From that former pastoral scene has emerged a heavily populated, highly developed community that is well served by major highways and nearby interstate corridors. You will find family-oriented neighborhoods with an abundance of medical and health care treatment centers here. Traffic can be challenging depending on the time of day and what direction drivers are headed but the multi-lanes and relatively high speed of the main thoroughfare, North Dale Mabry Highway, keeps things moving.

As growth and development continues to spread north, some of Tampa's newest residential areas are attracting families who seek spacious homes, gated communities and all of the amenities wanted within a convenient, well defined area. New Tampa is one of the largest residential areas in the city and is defined by its master-planned communities, like Cory Lake Isles, that feature modern homes and well groomed yards. Cory Lake Isles, one of Tampa's largest lake communities, is built around a 165-acre lake that is ideal for boating and water sports and boasts a 1,700-square-foot conservation preserve. Residents enjoy community pools, tennis courts, golf courses and jogging paths plus nearby major retailers, leading restaurants and trendy shops and boutiques.

Up and Coming Communities and Developments

Whether you are eager to locate your new home right away or opt to temporarily rent before selecting your new neighborhood, you may want to keep in mind the following projects and developments on the horizon:

ENCORE! ® expanded its resident-ready offerings from the first phase that opened in 2013. The Ella at ENCORE! is a mid-rise apartment building specifically suited for active seniors. Additional apartments will welcome singles, couples and families in 2014. The master-planned, mixed-use project is a private and public partnership that will create a vibrant community in an area bordering the downtown Tampa business district. When complete, the 40-acre, 12-block, energy-efficient retail, residential, cultural and recreational project will be home to 2,500 people.

Residences at the Riverwalk is a 36-story apartment building that will add 360 units to the downtown Tampa housing mix. It will rise north of Kennedy Boulevard, near the Straz Center for the Performing Arts.

Construction is slated to began in 2014 on SkyHouse Channelside, a 23-story, 320-unit apartment building that joins a number of residential towers already located in the Channel District that is bordered by downtown Tampa and Ybor City. Residents will likely take occupancy in 2015.

East Hillsborough will be the scene of significant commercial construction as work gets under way on a new 140,000-square-foot

Bass Pro Shop in Brandon and an Amazon warehouse fulfillment center to be built in Riverview. Jobs generated by both projects will likely spur housing demand in and, in turn, more residential development in those areas as well.

The ENCORE is a master-planned community that provides rental properties for singles, couples, families and seniors.

Getting to Know East Hillsborough County

East Hillsborough County is Tampa's premier bedroom community. The residential construction boom, inventory of existing homes and the availability of land, make this one of the most affordable areas to live. There is a development for every taste, from new homes with amenities, trails and golf courses, to houses with more acreage and a secluded environment. The price and quality of living, compared to other areas of the county, make East Hillsborough County the place to be.

Most of the population growth is occurring in communities like Riverview, Valrico, Apollo Beach, Ruskin, Plant City and Lithia. These are conveniently located near Brandon, the most densely populated part of this area.

A huge advantage to living in this area is access to the interstate corridor. I-4 runs east to west and accommodates commutes to Tampa or even the Lakeland or Orlando areas. From north to south, I-75 serves the majority of the new residential areas. These two interstates also connect with the Lee Roy Selmon Crosstown Expressway, a marvelous expressway that can quickly take you from Brandon to Tampa.

Gerardo Luna

As a real estate agent I chose this area because of the convenience of being so close to Tampa but separated from it at the same time. You can be in Tampa in just 20 minutes. You can buy fresh picked produce in nearby Plant City. Just a few miles down the road you can observe manatees in their natural habitat or enjoy accessing Tampa Bay from the Apollo Beach marina.

This extensive area offers residents a well-rounded lifestyle. The Westfield Brandon Mall is strategically located near I-4, the Crosstown and I-75. Its modern design includes nearly 200 stores, casual dining spots and full service restaurants.

East Hillsborough County is home to Brandon Regional Hospital, a 398-bed acute care facility that offers a number of specialized services including the Heart & Vascular Center, where the latest in cardiovascular surgery and minimally invasive surgical techniques are performed, the Behavioral Health Center, the Women's Center, which includes baby suites and a 22-bed neonatal intensive care unit, the Reflux Center and a designated Bariatric Center of Excellence.

Plant City retains its agriculture roots but also features lovely residential neighborhoods and historic sights. The downtown district has 185 preserved buildings originally constructed for residential, educational, or agricultural use that have been restored. Known as the Winter Strawberry Capital of the world, Plant City hosts the annual Florida Strawberry Festival, a 10-day event famous for a top musical entertainment, a midway filled with rides, and, of course, lots of delicious strawberries.

Apollo Beach is a growing community with direct access to I-75 and all that East Hillsborough County has to offer. The residential market offers waterfront properties and a master-planned community with multiple amenities.

Apollo Beach is well known for its estimated 55 miles of canals and marinas, access to Tampa Bay as well as for Tampa Electric Company's (TECO) power plant and the Manatee Viewing Center that is open November through April and includes a recently expanded viewing platform where everyone enjoys watching the dancing manatees.

Ruskin, located south of Apollo Beach, is primarily an agricultural community that recently expanded into suburban housing developments due to the convenient access to the I-75 corridor as well as Amazon's planned million-square-foot facility.

Ruskin is famous for their tomatoes, Cockroach Key Historic site and the A.P. Dickman House, which is on the U.S. National Register of Historic Places.

Riverview, located between Brandon and Apollo Beach, is where most of the recent residential growth has taken place. Infrastructure improvements to US 301 created a commercial boom in that area. A new mall and a new hospital are planned to serve the areas of Apollo Beach and Ruskin and accommodate future growth.

Valrico, Seffner, Bloomingdale area, Boyette area, Dover and even Fishhawk (located in Lithia) are considered part of the "Brandon area."

Being in this part of town makes going to Orlando and its attractions an easy task. You are literally in the middle of everything. If you want to go to the Gulf beaches, you are just an hour away.

East Hillsborough County is full of diversity and a strong sense of community that makes it unique. It has some of the area's highest graded schools and it's a great community for anyone to establish roots and cultivate friendships.

We have it all. The only thing we are missing is you. Please come visit us. We will be happy to have you.

GERARDO LUNA
Realtor/Photographer
www.gerardolunaphotographs.com

Utilities

City of Tampa residents receive a consolidated bill for three services: water, wastewater (sewer) and solid waste (refuse and recycling). More than 140,000 water meters located within a 211-square-mile service area measure monthly consumption levels.

Hillsborough County's Public Utility Department provides drinking water, wastewater treatment and disposal, solid waste collection and disposal and recycling services for residents in the unincorporated areas outside of the city limits. Tampa, Plant City and Temple Terrace are not part of the county's service area.

A rate schedule for those various county services shows that a typical single-family home uses about 300 gallons of water daily. An online water bill calculator estimates that the monthly cost based on that usage is $27.94. That includes a $4.31 per 1,000 gallon wastewater charge that is capped at 8,000 gallons per month for each single-family home. County residents are provided with two garbage pickups, one recycling pickup and one yard waste pickup each week.

Fees for county trash collection and disposal services are billed annually. In 2014, single family homes located in unincorporated areas paid $222.75 for service from January through December.

TECO, Tampa Electric, has been the area's primary source of electric power since 1899. The current service area covers 2,000 square miles within the West Central Florida area that is inhabited by more than one million people.

A 2013 rate increase saw average TECO residential monthly bills for 1,000 kilowatt-hours rise by $5.67 a month, or 5.5 percent, to $108.25 from the previous average of $102.58.

An Energy & Sustainability Report by Hillsborough County Government estimates an average family of four uses about 600 kilowatt hours of electricity per month, primarily for heating and cooling.

TECO contends its electric bills are 9% below the national average and reports 2014 residential bill totaling 1,000 kilowatt-hours usage was $109.61 (excludes franchise fees or applicable city taxes).

TECO People's Gas has provided Central Florida homes and business with natural gas for more than 115 years. Its residential rates in 2014 averaged $41.53 per household.

For wireless and landline phones, cable TV and internet service, the area's primary providers are Bright House Networks and Verizon.

Bright House is the nation's 6th largest owner and operator of cable systems and the second largest in Florida. Customers may subscribe to one, or more, of the following: video, high-speed data and phone services. Headquartered in New York, Verizon Communications Inc., operates the largest 4G LTE network in the nation and global service to more than 150 countries.

Taxes

There is no personal income tax in Florida. But you will pay a range of other taxes, depending on where you live and whether you conduct business here. Below is a breakdown of the major taxes compiled by the State of Florida:

- Sales tax rate is 6%.

- Corporations that do business and earn income in Florida must file a corporate income tax return (unless they are exempt).

- Florida Property Tax is based on market value as of Jan. 1st that year.

Counties have the discretion to levy local taxes in addition to those that the state collects. Hillsborough County is among those levying a local sales tax. The 7% sales tax collected by Hillsborough County is equal to the average for all 67 Florida counties.

Property taxes are assessed and collected by the Hillsborough County Property Appraiser. There is an online tax estimator that enables you to figure out what the annual tax will be on a property based on an average millage (tax) rate of 21 mills or $21 per thousand. For example, a Tampa home with a market value of $100,000 that qualified for the homestead exemption, may be assessed $1,087-$1,278.

The site cautions that the "estimate does not include non-ad valorem taxes that may be applicable to this property, such as assessments for roads, fire, garbage, lighting, drainage, water, sewer, or homeowner association fees."

The State of Florida allows everyone who owns and resides on real property that is their permanent residence as of Jan. 1 to receive a homestead exemption up to $50,000. The first $25,000 applies to all property taxes, including school district taxes. The additional $25,000 applies to the assessed value between $50,000-$75,000 and only to non-school taxes. Homeowners must apply for exemptions through their county property appraiser. The application is Form DR-501 and forms can be downloaded.

First-time filers will need to answer the following:

- Whose name or names were recorded on the title on Jan. 1?

- What is the street address of the property?

- Were you living in the dwelling on Jan. 1?

- Do you claim homestead in another county or state?

Feeling Safe in Tampa?

No city is immune from crime but Tampa seems to be successfully monitoring public areas and taking measures to better maintain security for residents and visitors alike.

Tampa's increasingly vibrant economy, retiree population and popularity as a travel destination can make it an attractive target for scam artists, thieves on the lookout for valuables left unguarded in cars, muggings and even more violent crimes. But the city seems to be following a statewide trend and managing to keep crime on the decline.

A forceful show of law enforcement personnel and resources utilized during the 2012 Republican National Convention held in Tampa provided local law enforcement with surveillance cameras strategically placed throughout the downtown area. Those cameras may be contributing to making the city safer by monitoring criminal activity and even identifying individuals suspected of committing crimes.

To look up criminal activity within a particular area of Tampa, the City of Tampa web site links to a crime mapping resource called RAIDS Online. Residents outside of the city can access information about what crimes occur and where they happen through the Hillsborough County Sheriff's Office internet-based crime information and mapping link.

For a breakdown of the types of crime that most commonly occur within the city and the county, the Hillsborough Community Atlas provides annual crime statistics.

The chances of becoming a victim of a violent crime in Tampa are just 1 in 161, slightly more than for Florida, which shows a 1 in 205 chance.

Healthcare and Medical Facilities

Tampa is well on its way to becoming increasingly well known for its world-class medical treatments and technology and state-of-the-art health care facilities.

The impact of our medical renaissance is such a vital component of Tampa's future that the Tampa Hillsborough Economic Development Corp. is positioning this area as a global leader in progressive health care.

That means living here will provide convenient access to some of the best places and practitioners for diagnosing, treating and curing serious injuries and life-threatening illnesses.

Highlights of Tampa's healthcare community include the following:

Moffitt Cancer Center is Florida's sole National Cancer Institute-designated comprehensive care center in Florida and among 41 nationwide. The designation acknowledges Moffitt's achievements in research, contributions to clinical trails, prevention and cancer control.

The main campus of Moffitt Cancer Center is located near the University of South Florida.

The $38 million, 90,000-square-foot University of South Florida's Center for Advanced Medical Learning and Simulation (CAMLS) located in downtown Tampa, is considered to be the largest facility of its kind. By combining high tech tools and simulation techniques, CAMLS provides state-of-the-art surgical training.

St. Joseph's Children's Hospital opened its Steinbrenner Children's Emergency/Trauma Center in late 2013 to better accommodate the demands of treating more than 45,000 children annually. The state-certified, level II pediatric trauma referral center is the busiest children's emergency center in the region.

This community also benefits from the major medical research conducted in area facilities. With the help of a healthy and well-established medical community, and its support industries, Tampa Bay residents receive top quality health care and medical services.

Hospitals and Health Care Providers

BayCare Health System. headquartered in Clearwater, is a community-wide, not-for-profit network of preventive, diagnostic and treatment centers and services that encompass non-profit hospitals, outpatient facilities and services ranging from imaging and labs to behavioral health and home health care. In 2014, BayCare welcomed a new Heart Institute at St. Joseph's Hospital. That 35,000-square-foot campus offers advanced, comprehensive cardiovascular care.

St. Joseph's Hospital, St. Joseph's Children's Hospital and St. Joseph's Women's Hospital are all part of the BayCare family and are located northwest of downtown Tampa, within close proximity of each other. St. Joseph's Hospital, with 870 beds, ranks as Tampa's second largest hospital. St. Joseph's Children's Hospital is recognized as the region's busiest children's emergency center. Other local BayCare Health System facilities include St. Joseph's Hospital - North in Lutz and South Florida Baptist Hospital , which offers full service care in Plant City.

Since opening in 1986, Moffitt Cancer Center has consistently been ranked among "America's Best Hospitals" for cancer care by U.S. News & World Report since 1999 while earning a worldwide reputation for quality care.

Contributing to the prevention and cure of cancer is the primary mission of this 206-bed, not-for-profit hospital. Its Cancer Center has one of the largest blood and bone marrow transplant programs in the Southeast, performing more than 400 transplants a year.

In addition to the main facility found near the University of South Florida campus, outpatient cancer care can also be accessed at a satellite location, the Moffitt Cancer Center at International Plaza. Construction of a new $74.2 million, 200,000-square-foot outpatient facility located less than a mile from the cancer center's main complex is expected to be completed by 2015.

Tampa General Hospital (TGH) is a private, not-for-profit 1,018-bed hospital located on Davis Islands. It is home to the region's only adult solid organ transplant center, Level 1 trauma center and burn unit. As one of Florida's largest hospitals, and among the region's largest employers, TGH has a distinguished history that includes the successful completion of the state's first heart transplant in 1985.

Tampa General Hospital consistently ranks among the leading hospitals in the country.

TGH is a state-certified comprehensive stroke center and its 32-bed, Neuroscience Intensive Care Unit is one of the largest on Florida's west coast. U.S. News & World Report named TGH the best hospital in this metropolitan area for 2013-14.

Established in 1927, TGH has served as the primary teaching hospital for the USF Health Morsani College of Medicine since the school's inception in the early 1970s and is the clinical site for associate, baccalaureate and graduate nursing programs for the University of South Florida, University of Tampa, Hillsborough Community College, St. Petersburg College and University of Florida.

James A. Haley Veterans' Hospital is a 415-bed hospital that also provides 118 beds at the nursing home care unit located on-site. A teaching hospital and a tertiary care facility, it is classified as a Clinical Referral Level 1 Facility. It was the first VA hospital to be designated as a Magnet Hospital, a national benchmark for excellence in nursing care.

The hospital consists of five Veterans Health Administration facilities (access points). Two are located in Tampa and New Port Richey, and three community-based outpatient clinics are found in Zephyrhills, Lakeland and Brooksville.

Shriners Hospital for Children Tampa specializes in caring for children requiring treatment for the following: orthopedic and neuromusculoskeletal conditions, burn and spinal cord injuries or cleft lip and palate procedures. This healthcare is provided without financial obligation to patients or families.

The Tampa location opened in 1985 and is one of 22 facilities of its kind in the U.S. Canada and Mexico.

CHAPTER 4
SHOPPING

From Big Malls to Boutiques, Home Decor to Designer Fashions

Shopping opportunities throughout the Tampa Bay area range from major retail outlets to specialty stores, luxury to low-cost goods and brand new to gently used merchandise.

No single mall offers it all, but area wide there is a huge array of major department stores, chic boutiques, sources for everything from sportswear to formalwear and stores stocking hardware to hard-to-find products.

There was a time when names like Neiman Marcus, Tiffany and Louis Vuitton couldn't be found in Tampa. Thanks to a growing population, and the increasing disposable income of residents and visitors alike, we are now on a first name basis with Henri Bendel, Tory Burch and Michael Kors. But that doesn't mean we don't just as eagerly swarm H&M or check out the clearance rack at DSW Shoes.

Sure, we know our designers and long for those red carpet moments. But, we also love the outdoors where we can fish, swim, sail, hike, bike and hunt. One of the biggest outdoors stores in the country, Bass Pro Shops, plans to expand to the Brandon area (east of Tampa) and open a 140,000-square-foot destination store.

Major brand names and shops that are tops in their category are a big part of the local retail scene. Shop for the latest technology at the Apple Store or create a customized closet for shoes, clothes and accessories at The Container Store.

Tampa may not start many fashion trends but it certainly knows which ones to follow and how to work those looks. Each fall a collection of runway events and style seminars, known as Fashion Week, celebrate collections created by local designers. One of the Tampa's leading style-makers is the aptly named Judy Tampa whose designs are carried in stores throughout the country and in Canada. Locally, you can find her latest creations at South Tampa's Deborah Kent's.

Whatever the size of your budget, there are plenty of places to find top quality household goods from kitchen utensils at Williams-Sonoma to secondhand home decor from the fine furniture collections showcased at Britton Plaza's The Missing Piece.

Fill a room or complete a house with smart looking furnishings that won't bust your budget from IKEA. Outfit your kitchen with top-of-the-line culinary tools at the Rolling Pin Kitchen Emporium or create the stylish kitchen or bathroom of your dreams at the place with the most fashionable faucets and sleekest sinks, Ferguson's located in South Tampa's Willow Design District.

When you don't have the time to run all around town, you'll probably find that Hyde Park Village boasts the best range of merchandise to meet your needs. This open-air collection of shops and restaurants is quite walkable. On weekends, it hosts special events ranging from a monthly farmer's market to craft beer festivals. Many of its stores are found only in Tampa, like Betty, with its casual but stylish women's fashions and home furnishings, but there are also familiar retail residents like Pottery Barn and Restoration Hardware.

For one of the most convenient retail collections where you can fill an eclectic shopping list, check out Walter's Crossing located at the intersection of North Dale Mabry Highway and I-275. Here you can browse for fashionable bargains at Nordstrom Rack, find stylish shoes at discount prices for the whole family at DSW, pick up your pet's favorite treats at PetSmart, re-stock the liquor cabinet at Total Wine & More, or get what is needed to build a liquor cabinet at Home Depot.

For haute couture and hot restaurants be sure to head for International Plaza. Here you can smartly outfit a home at the area's only Crate & Barrel Store or arm yourself with the latest Gucci handbag. The lively Bay Street area is an open-air section where locals love to flock for a post-shopping meal or show off their new outfits while dancing at Blue Martini.

You need it, you name it, you can find it somewhere in Tampa Bay.

International Plaza offers a mix of fashionable boutiques, major department stores, specialty shops and places to dine.

Grocery & Gourmet Shopping

The Tampa area offers a wonderful selection of places to shop for food. Florida's nearly year-round growing season provides a variety of fresh-picked produce; the nearby Gulf of Mexico is brimming with plenty of fresh seafood. And, local farmers and ranchers are making it abundantly easier for both professional chefs and local residents to purchase locally sourced foods.

Filling a shopping list has never been so convenient and so rich with choices. From multi-national stores to mom-and-pop shops, you can find an increasingly diverse range of products ranging from imported items and familiar brand names to organically grown produce, fresh-from-the-oven, gluten-free baked goods and farm fresh eggs.

Supermarkets, weekly and monthly farmer's markets, produce stands, specialty stores, gourmet grocers and stores that feature a wide selection of "green," or more natural foods and products, round out the retail outlets available throughout the area.

At the top of the food store chain is Publix Supermarkets, which is headquartered in Lakeland, FL and founded in 1930. This is the largest and fastest-growing employee-owned supermarket in the U.S. It's almost impossible to drive more than a few blocks in any direction, without passing a Publix or a Publix GreenWise Market that stocks all-natural and organic products. In addition to being prominent and dominant, the stores are known for outstanding family-friendly customer service.

Another grocery with deep ties to Florida is Winn-Dixie. The Jacksonville-Fl-based chain is a subsidiary of BI-LO Holdings, LLC, the 9th largest traditional supermarket chain in the nation, operating nearly 500 stores in Alabama, Florida, Georgia, Louisiana and Mississippi.

A relative newcomer to the local food shopping scene is The Fresh Market which began in North Carolina in 1982 but now has locations in 20 states, including two in Tampa, one in Clearwater and another in St. Petersburg. Whether buying ready-to-eat dishes or stocking up on basics, the choices are a bit more choice and the shelves are stocked with more out-of-the-ordinary brands and specialty items than more traditional groceries.

Whole Foods Market made its Tampa Bay debut 2007 and expanded to Carrollwood in 2012. Known for natural and organic foods and products – from soaps to soups to pet food and fresh seafood – Whole Foods appeals to the health conscious carnivore as well as to the strict vegan or vegetarian. Try not to shop hungry - there are many made-to-order and ready-to-eat foods, including a salad bar and hot food bar And, lots of free samples throughout the store may be too tempting to pass up.

Another recent, and extremely economical, addition to the list of grocers is ALDI. Since opening its first Central Florida location in 2008, this discount grocer has already sprouted up quickly with three locations in Tampa, two in Brandon, one in Plant City and six in Pinellas County. ALDI carries a fraction of what competitors stock and the inventory is predominantly private label but cost savings can be significant.

In South Tampa, a family-owned and operated market offers raw honey, cage-free eggs, raw milk plus a variety of fresh vegetables. The South Tampa Farm lacks a big flashy sign and weekly ad fliers but it boasts farm-fresh foods from a farm founded more than 35 years ago.

If really going to the source is more your style, Sweetwater Organic Farm hosts a Sunday market from November to May that is very popular with families. The urban organic farm and environmental education center operates a Community Supported Agriculture (CSA) membership program that lets people pay to receive a weekly share of the harvest.

Independent businesses that specialize in gourmet and healthy foods include Duckweed Urban Market in downtown Tampa and The Corner Store in Plant City. Duckweed Urban Market relocated from its original downtown location into the lobby of a nearby high-rise residential tower in 2013 making it easy for office workers and residents alike to buy craft beers, freshly squeezed juices, meats, sweets and many made-in-Tampa items like roasted coffee and honey. The Corner Store opened its doors in the historic downtown district of Plant City to provide seasonal produce and quality ingredients for home chefs. The owners, founders and creators of the concept incorporated locally sourced and re-purposed materials into the charming décor. They feature a made-from-scratch menu that offers a delicious selection of soups, salads and sandwiches. In addition to seasonings, sauces, produce and more sold at the store, it also stocks items crafted by local artists.

Eastern Hillsborough has lots of acreage dedicated to crops like strawberries and blueberries that invite the public out for dedicated u-pick times. But if you prefer picking up rather than picking, check out Parkesdale Farm Market, another Plant City fixture. It is said to be the largest strawberry and citrus market in the state. It's as popular for its fruits and vegetables as it is for the strawberry milkshakes, strawberry cookies and strawberry shortcake that is serves up on site.

Tampa's ethnic mix drives demand for specialty markets featuring a variety of cuisines. St. Petersburg's Mazzaro's Italian Market is considered a major destination for foodies and the ultimate shopping source for chefs. Under one sprawling roof is a wine and beer shop, cheese counter, butcher shop, bakery, freshly made pastas, coffee bar, fresh seafood section and more. Plan to spend a lot of time here to shop, eat and enjoy. Next-door is the large and lovely Casa di Mazzaro, which stocks cookware, housewares, teas and aprons to outdoor grilling utensils.

For something equally exotic, but a bit closer to home, explore the Oceanic Supermarket located on the outskirts of downtown Tampa. Tanks of live seafood, unfamiliar fresh produce, roasted duck and Oriental teas are just a sample of what awaits shoppers here. It is easy to feel as if you've been transported to Chinatown in San Francisco or New York while trying to decipher some of the store's signage and trying to determine just what those oddly shaped vegetables could possibly be or how they need to be prepared.

A favorite alternative to big box grocery stores are the various farmers' markets that set up weekly or monthly during much of the year. Typically, from fall through spring, vendors bring whatever is in season to designated areas for shoppers to select. The prices can be enticing, especially considering the quality and freshness of the produce. Many markets even offer fresh baked goods, private label hot sauces, artisan cheeses and much more. Bring a shopping bag, plenty of cash and arrive early for the best selection.

One of the most highly anticipated additions to the local retail mix is the arrival of California-based Trader Joe's making a grand entrance into this market with, not one, but two Tampa Bay locations, South Tampa and St. Petersburg. The popular shop is known for its eclectic mix of imported, private label and nicely priced foods and a good selection of well-priced wines, many which will be available here for the first time. Those in the know make sure to stock up during each visit to Trader Joe's because part of the adventure is its constantly changing inventory.

Major Shopping Malls

Tampa's Bay's large retail complexes range from enclosed to open-air and single-story to double-decker. All are filled with nationally known stores, chains and names as well as some only-in-Florida retailers. With movie complexes, sports bars and casual to fine dining options available at most malls, the opportunities to spend time - and money - while shopping, dining or being entertained are endless.

If one-stop shopping is your goal, check out the area's largest shopping complexes for the best variety of the latest fashions to leading beauty products, toys for girls and boys, athletic gear, keepsake jewelry to the latest, greatest electronics and cell phones.

International Plaza and Bay Street

This large, two-story shopping complex is complemented by Bay Street, an outdoor section lined with places to dine, drink and dance. New in 2014 is a Life Time Fitness facility offering fitness programs, spa treatments, recreational activities for children and nutritional meals to promote healthy lifestyles. This centrally located shopping destination is located near Tampa International Airport and Raymond James Stadium and connected to the Renaissance Tampa International Plaza Hotel.

Life Time Fitness opened its first Central Florida location at International Plaza

The Shoppes at Wiregrass

Wear - or be sure to buy - comfortable walking shoes when making your way through this open-air, 850-000-square-foot collection of retail and restaurant establishments. Its collection of anchor stores includes Dillard's, JCPenney and Macy's. If you work up an appetite walking around, there are nearly two dozen eateries offering frozen yogurt and wood-fired pizza to Philly steaks and sushi.

Westfield Brandon

The sprawling mall is bordered by multiple shopping centers making it one of the area's busiest places to park and among the most congested places to shop. But there's something to be said for having major department stores like Dillard's and Sears, leading discount stores like Target, and specialty stores like Bed Bath & Beyond so close together when you have a long list of gifts to buy.

Westfield Citrus Park

This mall seems to have it all. Think large-scale and long walks from end-to-end. It offers shoppers five anchor stores, a multi-plex movie theater, several restaurants, a food court and even Atomic Tattoos for piercings and body art.

Westshore Plaza

The area's first fully enclosed and air-conditioned shopping center, Westshore remains a popular shopping spot and place to see first-run movies at the AMC multi-plex. The food court is a great place for a quick bite or a healthy snack. For full service dining, select from Seasons 52, Mitchell's Fish Market, Maggiano's Little Italy and P.F. Chang's.

Hyde Park Village

This picturesque, open-air collection of stores, restaurants and a movie theater is nestled in the neighborhood of Hyde Park. Restaurants and shops blend locally-owned, independent businesses with well known national and regional chains.

Shopping for Bargains and Good Causes

Consignment, second hand and thrift shops offer an ever-changing selection of clothes, coats, purses, accessories, home decor and more throughout the year.

LifePath Hospice Thrift Stores

Sales of gently used to brand new clothes, furniture, books and other items support LifePath Hospice patient and family programs.

The Spring Boutique

Sales of donated clothing, furniture and household goods from two locations provide shelter and support for victims of domestic abuse.

GoodWill Industries - Suncoast Inc.

Sales of new and used clothes, furniture, household items and more support employment services and training programs for people with barriers to employment.

Salvation Army

Sales of furniture, clothing, household goods and more fund adult rehabilitation centers that offer housing, work, group and individual therapy.

Consignment, Secondhand, Name Brand

Mosh Post Designer Consignment Boutique

High-end purses, shoes and apparel guaranteed to be authentic.

Plato's Closet

Gently worn top-name brands and on-trend clothes for men and women.

The Missing Piece

Consignment shop features furnishings for every room and any lifestyle.

Triage Consignment Showcase

Family owned and operated consignment shop specializes in upscale women's clothing and home furnishings.

Play It Again Sports

Multiple locations throughout the Tampa area specialize in new and used sports and fitness equipment.

Shopping for clothes at Triage Consignment Showcase

Vintage, Classic and Retro Clothing & Household Goods

Boots, wigs, clothes, furniture and more can be found at Squaresville.

La France

This Ybor City store offers a stylish array of men's and women's fashions from throughout the ages, think Gatsby to the go go days of disco.

Sherry's YesterDAZE Vintage Clothing & Antiques

Located in Seminole Heights, this is where to go for fun to funky furniture, fine to costume jewelry and clothes from the late 1800s to early 1990s for men and women.

Squaresville Vintage & New Clothing, Retro Home Decor

To-die-for tie dye shirts, Elvis memorabilia, wild wigs and all things rock 'n roll plus furnishings for that 1950s feel and flair.

New to Re-Purposed, Recycled and Salvaged Furnishings, Lighting Fixtures & More

Blue Moon Trading Co.

One-of-a-kind pieces will highlight any room in your home. You'll find new merchandise from top names as well as pieces that have been re-purposed or custom built.

Magnolia Inspiring Interiors

Located in a restored 1923 grocery and pharmacy, discover everything from delicate jewelry to fine furnishings and original art to seasonal decorations that add fun and flair to any interior.

MarketPlace Interiors

Antique, vintage and new furniture are creatively showcased using vignettes created by various interior designers. There's the 4,000-square-foot indoor space plus an outdoor area for fountains, statues and benches. Located in the Willow Design District. www.addisondicus.com/info/design-center

Custom pieces to re-purposed items from Blue Moon create one-of-a-kind interior designs.

Schiller's Architectural and Design Salvage

Source for replacement home design or reclaimed home decor elements that can be used to construct a work-in-progress or create a new look with vintage elements.

Books, Magazines, Music and More

Barnes & Noble

Bestsellers, broad range of topics and current newspapers and magazines are part of the expansive inventory featured here. Curl up in a chair and sip something from the in-store café while you browse.

Inkwood Books

This local independent bookstore stocks new books, regularly hosts author events and can accommodate readers of all ages and all interests. It is located in a former house in the South Howard (SoHo) area of the city.

Inkwood Books is an independent bookstore located in Tampa's SoHo neighborhood.

Old Tampa Book Company

Like its name implies, this is the place to hunt for used, rare and out-of-print books with many nicely priced. This street-front shop is centrally located in downtown Tampa.

The Bookstore at the Oxford Exchange

This curated collection of classic to contemporary books covers a wide spectrum of subjects that include fiction, travel, history, science, medicine and business.

Haslam's Book Store

Located in St. Petersburg, this is Florida's largest new and used bookstore. John and Mary Haslam first opened it in 1933 and the business continues to be operated by a third generation of family members.

Banana's

This long-standing St. Petersburg source for music, movies and more fills 17,000 square feet – spread over two stores - with its vast musical collection. Rolling Stone Magazine ranks it among the top record stores in the country.

Oxford Exchange near downtown Tampa offers a bookstore, a retail area with home decor to fashionable jewelry, a restaurant and both a coffee and tea counter.

Mojo Books & Music

A rare independent used book and record store, it also operates a coffee and tea bar on-site along with offering a selection of posters, T-shirts and other memorabilia.

Sound Exchange

Three Tampa Bay locations feature new and used CDs, DVDs, video games, vinyl records, books and select stereo equipment.

More Shopping Trip Tips

Museums, attractions and non-profits throughout the Tampa Bay area generally feature gift shops stocked with books, jewelry, apparel, crafts and other items that can't be found at more traditional stores. Consider the Tampa Bay History Museum, Henry B. Plant Museum, Big Cat Rescue, Tampa Museum of Art, Florida Aquarium and other similar non-profits when looking for a special gift.

Farmer's markets are most often associated with food but can also be great sources for handmade items ranging from woven baskets to wood crafts and scented soaps to original paintings. Likewise, that's also true for annual festivals, arts shows and other special events.

Costco, Sam's Club and BJ's Wholesale Club are membership warehouses in the Tampa Bay area offering electronics to pet food, automotive supplies to cosmetics. But their big claim to fame would be the ability to buy in bulk.

Weekend garage sales and flea markets can be fun for those who enjoy the art of the hunt. Flea markets tend to operate throughout the year and through all kinds of weather. When someone invites you "saling" for the weekend they don't mean boating. They mean hitting neighborhoods to check for signs announcing "Multi-Household Yard Sale." Check online or local newspapers for listings for Friday, Saturday and Sunday yard sales and go early to get the best selection. If one-strop shopping is more your thing, the Big Top Flea Market in North Tampa is said to be the biggest and best of its kind, occupying more than 36 acres accommodating hundreds of vendors.

Filling You in on Fashion Finds

The Tampa Bay region is filled with shopping, retail and a love for fashion, from Home Shopping Network, HSN, and International Plaza and Bay Street, to the numerous boutiques located throughout the region.

Nancy Vaughn

HSN corporate headquarters is located in St. Petersburg and their campus hosts leading national and international fashion, accessory and beauty products and personalities, including: American Glamour by Badgley Mischka, Betsy Johnson, Diane Gilman, Joy Mangano, and more. In addition, HSN brings celebrity power to the region through its collaborations with everyone from Mariah Carey to Rhonda Shear. Overall, the region boasts more than 20+ malls and shopping centers, plus, Tampa Bay is in comfortable proximity to Ellenton Premium Outlets near Sarasota, providing even more opportunities to shop and save.

Such esteemed outlets as the New York Times salute Tampa for its hidden shopping gems, encouraging local shoppers to feed their vintage cravings at a variety of consignment shops including: Ybor City's La France, MISRED Outfitters in downtown St. Petersburg, Revolve Clothing Exchange and Sherry's YesterDaze Vintage in Seminole Heights. You can buy, sell or trade at many of these shops and find garments from decades ago or gently used labels of today. If you're looking for luxury clothing at a discount, you can try A&A Boutique. You will need to travel a little north of Tampa to Wesley Chapel where labels like Chanel,

Alexander McQueen, Louis Vuitton, and Prada are readily found on the racks. For shoppers who don't want to commit, the latest styles and leading designers area available in abundance at SoHo's Lending Luxury. There you can rent your next lavish outfit.

Fashion designers from various parts of the U.S. participate in the annual Tampa Bay Fashion Week held each fall that is marked by a series of runway shows, boutique vendor opportunities, fashion seminars, styling sessions and parties. This event brings talented fashion and accessories designers to Tampa Bay to showcase their work for local, regional and national retail buyers and boutique owners as well as style conscious consumers.

In addition, local business partners, aspiring models and community members have an opportunity to get a firsthand look at styles displayed by these fashion trendsetters and become inspired by the creativity and positive, high-fashion and artistic energy, that make this week a major event.

There definitely is an emerging local fashion scene that highlights the region's homegrown fashion and accessories design talent.

Tampa Bay-based fashion designers include the following: Rhonda Shear of Rhonda Shear Intimates, Essence Flowers of Essence Flowers Swim, Kimberly Hendrix of k.hendrix, Rogerio Martins, Sandra Hagen and more. The various designers specialize in a range of garments from couture to ready-to-wear.

Essence Flowers has designed for various NFL teams, including the Tampa Bay Buccaneers, while k.hendrix produces eco-friendly gowns seen on the red carpet in Hollywood. Shoppers can have their own, custom-made garment created by fashion design talents who reside in our region. Imagine walking away with a one-of-a-kind creation.

In addition, various other fashion industry players, including hair/make-up artists, fashion stylists, photographers and more, also reside in the region and contribute to the growing interest and influence of Tampa Bay fashion. There are two post-education schools that support the industry: The Art Institute of Tampa and the International Academy of Design & Technology.

If you're looking for some style and great shopping in Florida, Tampa Bay should be on your list. It's a Florida must-have and a great accessory to the fashion industry and shopping scene!

NANCY VAUGHN
White Book Agency
www.whitebookagency.com

CHAPTER 5
THINGS TO DO

Tampa loves to have fun, get outdoors, throw parties and just generally celebrate what's great about this area.

That can happen in many ways, including honoring its Italian heritage during Festa Italiana, turning the Hillsborough River green for St. Patrick's Day, paying a tongue-in-cheek homage to Halloween with Gauvaween or undergoing invasion by hundreds of rowdy pirates who annually sail to the city's shores during Gasparilla Pirate Fest. It's Tampa's take on Mardi Gras that's distinguished by parades, floats, free beads and costumed revelers.

St. Patrick's Day is marked by the temporary transformation of the Hillsborough River

This is also a place where people love to make the most of being outdoors. With water, water everywhere, many more sunny than grey days and lots of trails to run, ride, rollerblade and hike, Tampa offers a multitude of ways to seek entertainment, exercise and enjoyment.

There's sure to be something happening year round but most major annual events occur from fall through spring to avoid the heat, rain, humidity and possibility of storms that can hamper attendance during summer.

Even native Floridians have their limits when it comes to weathering the weather. Still, hardly a weekend arrives without heralding some arts event, a new theatrical performance or annual celebration, like the Florida State Fair, concert in the park or some other crowd-pleasing activity.

The Florida State Fair is one of Tampa's most popular winter events

Both the weather and wealth of natural beauty make it irresistible to get outdoors for much of the year, whether to enjoy a picnic, paddle a canoe or kayak along the waterfront, participate in group rides with the area's popular bike peddling groups or compete for real, or for real fun, while running any of the many local race events.

Not quite so inclined to be quite so active? Cheer from the stands at a professional sports event, call for an encore at an opera or classical music concert, play a round at local golf courses, call the shots at tennis courts or set sail for a sunset cruise. And, that's just a few of the ways we like to play.

Golfers enjoy year-round access to the links throughout the Tampa area

The mix of things to do, places to go and special events to see, and be seen is expansive but not necessarily expensive. Many activities are free, require only a modest admission price or offer advance ticket purchase discounts.

Sporting Life

There's no shortage of professional sports here or any sorts of sports, for that matter. The region is home to the NFL's Tampa Bay Buccaneers football team, NHL's Tampa Bay Lightning hockey team, MLB's Tampa Bay Rays baseball team, NASL's Tampa Bay Rowdies soccer team and Arena Football's Tampa Bay Storm.

Major League Baseball spring training camps held locally include the New York Yankees at Tampa's Steinbrenner Field, the Philadelphia Phillies in Clearwater and the Toronto Blue Jays in Dunedin.

Collegiate sports schedules are offered by both the University of South Florida (USF) and the University of Tampa (UT).

Two post-season college football bowl games call Tampa Bay home. The former Beef 'O' Brady's Bowl/St. Petersburg Bowl is held late December at Tropicana Field in downtown St. Petersburg and features a bowl-eligible team from the Big East Conference competing with one from Conference USA.

The Outback Bowl is played in Raymond James Stadium on New Year's Day and pits teams from the SEC and Big Ten Conference. Ray Jay, as it is commonly referred to, is also the home field for the Buccaneers and the NCAA USF Bulls. Ray Jay has hosted two Super Bowls, in 2001 and 2009. But the first two Super Bowls held in Tampa were in 1984 and 1991 and were played at Ray Jay's predecessor, the former Tampa Stadium/Houlihan's Stadium/Big Sombrero.

In addition, we serve up a year-round calendar of amateur, youth and premier sports competitions. Ranging from Dragon Boat racing events to NCAA Final Four basketball games, these special events bring athletes from around the world to the area.

For information about upcoming athletic events, the Tampa Bay Sports Commission provides news about everything from international wakeboard competitions to NCAA championships being held in the Tampa Bay area.

Heart for the Arts

Our lively local performing and visual arts scene includes galleries, museums, opera companies, touring productions of Broadway hits, local theatrical groups and indoor and outdoor concert venues attracting major musical groups, solo artists and rock bands to top DJs who do their thing at Raymond James Stadium, the Tampa Bay Times Forum, where the NHL Lightning compete, MIDFLORIDA Credit Union Amphitheatre and the USF Sun Dome, to name a few venues.

One of the most popular ways to see a diverse group of musical acts is during the annual Florida Strawberry Festival in Plant City. An open-air stadium hosts top talent for ticket prices that can range from free to double digits. The yearly celebration of Plant City's world famous strawberry crop has been country strong for years but now offers a blend of performers appealing to a wider range of musical tastes and ages. Mixed in with Little Big Town, The Band Perry and Oak Ridge Boys are groups like Styx and performers like Brenda Lee.

Plant City produces the world's leading strawberry crop each winter

For a fun way to enjoy that next big blockbuster, independent or foreign film, head for the historic, beautifully ornate, Tampa Theatre in downtown Tampa. The Baroque-style film house was proclaimed "one of the world's most beautiful theaters" by the BBC in 2013. Best known for showing classic to contemporary movies, live entertainment occasionally fills the bill there as well. Among past performers are Arlo Guthrie, David Byrne and Colbie Caillat, Jimmy Fallon and Andrew Dice Clay. The 1926 movie theatre offers backstage-to-balcony tours and music performed live on its Mighty Wurlitzer just before the start of most movies.

The Tampa Theatre ranks among the most beautiful theaters in the world

The David A. Straz Center for the Performing Arts boasts one of the biggest and most diverse entertainment arrays in Florida with its straight-from-Broadway touring productions of Tony-award winning plays and musicals, Florida Orchestra concerts, elaborate productions of top operas, world-class classical musicians, Grammy-award winning artists, ballet troupes, modern dance companies and much more that populate any - or all - of its five theaters on almost a nightly basis. Theaters range from an intimate 130-seat venue to the 2,610-seat Carol Morsani Hall.

Downtown has evolved into a cultural hub for the Tampa arts scene because of its collection of museums, historic sites and theatrical facilities.

Just across the Hillsborough River is the University of Tampa where the Henry B. Plant Museum is housed. The Plant Museum preserves the original look and lifestyle that made the former Tampa Bay Hotel a high-end, winter resort when it opened in 1891. In addition to recreating the decor of the guest rooms, the museum hosts special exhibits typically tied to Tampa's past.

The Straz Performing Arts Center brings dazzling entertainment to downtown Tampa year round

Closer to the downtown core is an outstanding collection of arts and entertainment facilities that include intriguing exhibits featured at the Florida Museum of Photographic Arts. The Tampa Museum of Art is a stunning structure with an even more impressive ability to attract exceptional artworks to its galleries. Completing that cultural scene is the playful Glazer Children's Museum and the interactive and informative Tampa Bay History Museum.

Tampa's got talent. The professional artists who live and work locally are living proof, occasionally opening up their studios for special tours or fundraising events best illustrate that. Susan Gott is one local resident and award-winning glass artist whose work has been commissioned and collected worldwide. Bleu Acier is a studio owned by a talented couple who are both renowned artists in their own right: Erika Greenberg-Schneider and Dominique Labauvie. She is a master printmaker and he is an accomplished sculptor and painter. Their live/work space is also a venue for showcasing works by other esteemed artists.

The Gasparilla Festival of the Arts is not only Tampa's best known and best-attended arts-related event but it is one of the highest-rated outdoor shows of its kind in the country. This is a juried show offering serious prize money for fine art and fine crafts.

Florida Museum of Photographic Arts in downtown Tampa

Many fine galleries represent local to international artists. When it comes to special exhibits, Gallery 221 at the Hillsborough Community College Campus in Tampa, is greatly admired for curating really creative art events that have built quite a following, generating crowds at its opening events. The exceptional exhibits range from folk art to three-dimensional pieces throughout the year, frequently showcasing artists with ties to the local area.

The Arts Council of Hillsborough County is an excellent resource for information about upcoming events, venues, classes and workshops related to the arts.

Culinary Arts

Tampa is becoming increasingly known as a food scene that features a mix of landmark restaurants, farm-to-fork dining spots, movable feasts served up by food trucks and newcomers to the dining scene as well as new concepts that grew into global brands.

Food trucks from throughout Florida and as far away as Canada helped set a world record in 2013

Want to catch the next celebrity chef? The Culinary Arts and Design School at the Art Institute of Tampa operates "The Tutored Chef" restaurant that is open to the public for lunch and dinner when classes are in session. Watch chefs at work in the kitchen through the clear glass windows that let guests observe while they dine on delightfully delicious dishes created before their eyes. A big plus is that prices are well below what comparable fare would fetch at comparable restaurants.

A philosophy of *"if you can make it here you can make it anywhere,"* continues as other newcomers extend their own brand of hospitality statewide and out-of-state. The Tampa Bay area has proved to be a proving ground for new restaurant concepts. Outback Steakhouse restaurants, part of the Bloomin' Brands family, got its start here and the history of Hooters can be traced to its first location in Clearwater.

Restaurants boasting the deepest roots in Tampa's culinary development are the acclaimed Bern's Steak House and Columbia Restaurant. Bern's, is one of a kind, world-famous for its aged steaks, comprehensive wine collection and decadent array of some 50 desserts as well as more than 1,000 dessert wines and spirits served in the Harry Waugh Dessert Room. It has been a favorite of world leaders, celebrities and the rich and famous for decades as well as a popular spot for locals since 1956. Bern's is best known for its steaks but offers a wide selection of dishes, including 21 types of caviar. Wine cellar and kitchen tours are available to all guests and both offer impressive behind-the-scenes looks at this legendary operation.

A more contemporary, seasonal style of cuisine is served at SideBern's a separate but related dining venture that is located on the same street as

The Tutored Chef restaurant is located on the campus of the Art Institute of Tampa

Bern's. Since joining SideBern's in 2008, Chef Chad Johnson has been honored as a James Beard semi-finalist for Best Chef. He continues to flex his culinary muscles while dividing his time at the latest addition to the Laxer family empire, Elevage at The Epicurean Hotel. The Epicurean is a 137-room boutique-style hotel that includes its signature restaurant, a patisserie, 40-seat culinary theater, spa, wine store and rooftop bar. Opened in late 2013, the hotel is directly across the street from Bern's.

[Bern's and the new Epicurean Hotel are both located in Tampa's SoHo district]

The original Columbia Restaurant, located in Ybor City, is a two-story, beautifully ornate landmark building spanning an entire city block. Founded in 1905 by Cuban immigrant Casimiro Hernandez Sr., it is the oldest restaurant in Florida and the largest Spanish restaurant in the world.

The Columbia now has seven distinctive locations in Florida including a cafe at Tampa International Airport. It has been owned and operated by the same family for five generations and remains a favorite destination dining spot for families, couples and groups to enjoy, not only outstanding food and a celebrated selection of more than 1,000 wines presented on a 240-plus page wine list, but also great entertainment. Flamenco/Spanish classical dance performances are available exclusively at the Ybor City restaurant nightly, except Sundays.

Flamenco dancers perform at the Columbia Restaurant in Ybor City

Not content to rest on this landmark restaurant's laurels, one of the patriarchs of the Columbia Restaurant, Richard Gonzmart, has created a new concept opening in an historic building located on the outskirts of downtown Tampa in 2014. Ulele will honor the original Native American Indian inhabitants of this area by fusing elements from their culture with other cultural influences and utilizing indigenous ingredients from local waters and farms to create a new, different and dynamic dining experience.

The Tampa area has not always been noted for haute cuisine but that is changing as restaurants and chefs gain professional recognition, garnering James Beard nominations and attracting Food Network TV crews shooting on-location segments at local favorites like Taco Bus, which grew from a single food truck to multiple bus-themed dining spots featuring authentic Mexican food. Other nationally televised segments featured Skipper's Smokehouse, known for its, rustic setting and Florida seafood. Its popular Skipperdome features live music from all genres and performers from all over the globe.. Another featured food spot is Tampa Bay Brewing Company, a family-owned on-site microbrewery and restaurant that incorporates many of its craft beers into the dishes it serves.

The on-going popularity of food trucks reached a milestone in 2013. The Florida State Fairgrounds in Tampa hosted a one-day event billed as the "World's Largest Food Truck Rally" that attracted mobile chefs from around the state and across the country to Tampa to set a new record of 99 trucks.

Craft beer and brewpubs continue to come on strong locally as new breweries, tasting rooms and beer-inspired dining spots cater to micro-brew fans. Cigar City Brewing continues to reign as the area's leader for its award-winning brews. Its growing brand now includes a brewpub as well as the first airport brewpub in the country at Tampa International Airport.

Craft distilleries are now starting to crop up around the area as small batch production facilities of premium to flavored spirits gain in popularity. Some feature Florida-grown ingredients and others specialize in signature lines of rums, vodkas, whiskeys and more. Twisted Sun Rum is one of the new brands and will likely launch the first Tampa-based production facility with a projected opening in 2014.

Cigar City Brewpub combines Cuban, Southern and Italian cuisine with Cigar City Brewery craft beers

Wonderful Dining Choices: From Paella to Pad Thai and from Steak to Sushi

I still remember smarting when a comic declared Tampa had every kind of cuisine as long as it was "fried." That quip certainly doesn't hold up today. Tampa is a virtual skillet full of culinary delights where robust appetites have incubated nationally recognized chains and trends.

Mary Scourtes

Some of our native-born restaurants earn us coast-to-coast kudos. The Columbia has served Spanish sangria, paella, salteado and an olive-rich, 1905 salad for more than 100 years. The Gonzmart family

82

recently added Ulele, an eatery and brew pub, in a historic Water Works building.

Bern's Steak House raises the stakes for steaks. Cut-to-order, aged steaks are precisely defined by weight and thickness. To please the most astute oenophile its wine list, an encyclopedia-of-the-vine, catalogs more than 6,000 varieties in a cellar housing a half-million bottles. A few vintages stretch back to the 1850s.

Shula's, Eddie V's, Capitol Grill, Ocean Palm, Ruth's Chris Steak House, Flemings Prime Steakhouse, and Council Oak Steak & Seafood at the Seminole Hard Rock Hotel are part of the city's high-end steak playground.

Kevin and Karyn Kruszewski's Pane Rustica and chef Brett Gardiner at Pelagia at the Renaissance Tampa International Plaza, take Italian cooking to new heights. Armani's celebrates the most scenic views of Old Tampa Bay from its 14th floor dining rooms. Mise en Place Chef Marty Blitz annually earns top honors at his sophisticated, south Tampa mainstay in the shadows of the University of Tampa minarets.

Fervid partisans flock to the new boys (or girls) on the block too, such as Edison, where star chef Jeannie Pierola reigns. Michelle and Greg Baker's The Refinery and Suzanne and Roger Perry's Dough and Datz gastro pub offer seasonal inspirations.

Castillo's joins many cherished family-owned, West Tampa ethnic eateries where a sausage-stuffed beef boliche, ropa de Viejo, and meaty, deviled crabs reveal classic tastes.

Despite a dust up with Miami, Tampa is the home of the real Cuban sandwich because Ybor City's early bricklayers flattened these "mixto" sandwiches between hot bricks to sear the crust, melt cheese and meld flavors. These peppercorn-speckled Genoa salami, baked ham, pork and Swiss cheese sandwiches on crusty, Cuban bread are Numero Uno in our Cigar City. Travelers stock up with a cooler full before leaving town.

After year-round relaxing rounds of golf or tennis, locals love take-out from Wright's Gourmet House, started 40 years ago by Marjorie and Pete Wright. Their Cuban sandwiches are the gold standard, taking first place – almost forever - in The Tampa Tribune's annual Cuban sandwich contest that I had the pleasure of judging for many years.

Louis Pappas' Market Cafes draw in devotees of moussaka, pastitsio, baklava and all tastes Greek.

Indulge in hot bird's eye peppers, lemongrass, kaffir lime and galangal root-scented salads, soups and stir-fries at Thai Island, Royal Palace and Jasmine Thai. You'll also admire the spread at the Wat Mongkolratanaram (about a half-mile from U.S. 41 on the banks of the Palm River). Nicknamed "Wat Tampa," a flurry of temple volunteers participate in a mind-blowing cook-a-thon each Sunday.

Chinese, Indian, Vietnamese, Lebanese, Japanese, Ethiopian and others help make us a micro United Nations of cuisines. No surprise the International Indian Film Academy hosted its 2014 "Bollywood" ceremony here.

Outdoor markets put on in downtown, Hyde Park, Seminole Heights and Ybor City are where friendly faces offer samples and introduce you to not-so-common meat, vegetarian and organic fare.

Assorted lunch wagons, taco trucks and dinner cantinas satisfy the locals and the phenomenally popular meals-on-wheels park all around town, at farmers markets and at Food Truck Rallies.

Indulge in key lime pie under a blanket of meringue or dolled up with whipped cream. Mike's Pies does an award-winning, killer version and his Heath Bar Pie, Reese's Peanut Butter and turtle cheesecake are also worthy.

Rock the yacht with a 360-degree-view of Tampa Bay while sipping cocktails, then enjoy dinner, dancing and fireworks aboard the StarShip Yacht.

Fall easily into an eat-drink-and-party mantra with Tampa's variety. Your taste buds will dance all the way home.

MARY D. SCOURTES
Former newspaper food critic and food editor and currently a freelance writer for local and national publications.

Spectacular Points of View

Enjoy a sunrise or sunset run along Bayshore Boulevard, the world's longest, continuous sidewalk that winds along the waterfront for more than four miles. It's quite a sight to watch the tides of people go by night and day while walking dogs, pushing strollers, riding bikes, roller blading or leisurely strolling. And, it's a wonderful vantage point for watching birds diving into the water and dolphins swimming by.

The Tampa Riverwalk is a paved, pedestrian friendly stretch that winds along and around downtown's waterfront. This urban pathway borders the business district and runs from the Channel District past the Tampa Bay History Center and Tampa Bay Forum and along the channel that leads to the Tampa Convention Center. From there it continues to Curtis Hixon Waterfront Park that borders the Tampa Museum of Art, Glazer Children's Museum and Florida Photography Museum before continuing on to the Straz Performing Arts Center.

One of the newest dedicated scenic stretches for walkers and bikers is a paved path that parallels the Courtney Campbell Causeway connecting Tampa with Clearwater and Safety Harbor. The Courtney Campbell Trail is a scenic stretch spanning Tampa Bay that is off limits to cars and fishing and represents the first phase of a project that will eventually extend to connect trails in both Hillsborough and Pinellas counties. The four-mile-long, 16-foot-wide trail rises 45 feet above the water to provides breathtaking views.

Perks of Parks

One of the many perks of living here is the abundance of city and county parks. Curtis Hixon Waterfront Park in downtown Tampa is one of the area's most popular venues for musical groups, food festivals, seasonal activities, like the ice skating rinks that pops up during the holidays, and special events.

Plenty of public parks and playgrounds are open year round. Whether you want to reserve a site for a family picnic, watch your children play in the water-themed splash pad or swim in the pool or take a scenic hike, free city parks provide endless fun and good exercise.

County parks generally require a modest admission fee particularly if plans include launching a boat or camping overnight. Youth sports leagues and special camps and programs are also available but may require fees and registration.

View from Picnic Island Park located in Port Tampa

Area Attractions

While people travel from around the globe to enjoy these only-in-Tampa attractions, they are available year round for those who live here.

Busch Gardens began as a brewery and a garden spot filled with exotic birds. Birds are still part of the theme park's "residents" but beer is no longer being brewed there. Instead major thrill rides, state-of-the-art roller coasters, all sorts of exotic animals, live entertainment and a children's area designed with a Sesame Street theme, make this family-friendly attraction popular for all ages. The 297-acre park is considered one of the country's premier zoos with more than 12,000 animals. It also caters the thrill-ride enthusiasts who enjoy dropping from significant heights while traveling and exhilarating speeds.

Nearby Busch is the largest science center in the Southeast, the Museum of Science and Industry which has more than 450 hands-on exhibits incorporating scientific principals in fun, fascinating ways. Kids in Charge! is a designated area for youngsters, 12 and under, that has age-appropriate activities within a bright, light filled building. Recent additions to MOSI include the popular Sky Trail Ropes Course that invites adventurous types to test their skills of balance - and their ability to remain calm - while they climb and cross ropes, blocks and narrow tracks well above ground or go for the fast track and use the zip line to return to ground level.

Lowry Park Zoo earns high marks for family fun and provides fascinating looks at all types of animals in specially designed exhibits that eschew cages. More than 1,000 animals from around the world, as well as throughout Florida, are housed in natural habitats found within the nearly 60-acre site. The zoo is also home to a hospital for injured or ill manatees rescued from the wild, brought there to be treated and healed, before being returned to their natural habitat. Visitors can actually watch these enchanting, endangered creatures from a below water level viewing area that puts people face-to-face with manatees.

Lowry Park Zoo features a below-water viewing area that provides a perfect place to watch manatees in their natural habitat

Another free site to check out manatees is the Manatee Viewing Center, perched along the edge of Tampa Bay in Apollo Beach. Visit the open-air decks that lookout over the water during cold weather. The saltwater that originates in Tampa Bay is warmed as it flows through the Big Bend Power Station TECO facility. When the clean water is discharged back into the bay, the temperature provides critical protection from cold water for manatees, drawing them close to the shore for easy viewing.

Within viewing distance of the downtown Tampa Skyline and the Port Tampa Bay cruise ship terminals is the splashy Florida Aquarium, that features an outdoor water fun zone for youngsters and fascinating ways to view underwater worlds occupied byotters to alligators and from stingrays to moray eels, all within the 250,000-square-foot facility.

Rounding out the activities roster offered around the area is the Seminole Hard Rock Hotel & Casino, which ranks among the world's largest gambling and gaming establishments, and Tampa Bay Downs, a thoroughbred race track that has been a Tampa institution for nearly 90 years.

Cold weather draws manatees to the warm waters and makes them easy to spot from the Manatee Viewing Center in Apollo Beach

The Seminole Hard Rock Hotel & Casino offers fine dining, musical entertainment and ranks among the largest gambling and gaming establishments worldwide

CHAPTER 6

FROM PRE-K TO POST GRAD: CHILDCARE AND EDUCATION

Tampa has a lot to offer families. Deciding where to live, what schools to attend and whether any sort of day care is needed are critical factors that families must consider when determining whether to make Tampa their new home.

Infant and Toddler Care

Based on nationwide averages of childcare rates, DayCareMatch.com ranks Tampa among the least expensive cities for costs associated with a toddler attending a site-based care facility for five days a week. In 2013, the average weekly rate in Tampa totaled $241 for the care of a single child, according to the site.

Of course, that rate can vary according to the level of childcare service provided. Types of service may be more or less depending on whether the caregiver is to look after an infant or if older children require after school care. Whether supervision is needed for a half- to full-day as well as what, if any, additional services may be needed, like meals and transportation, will also factor into the equation. With so many variables to consider, it can be confusing and time-consuming to make realistic comparisons. Fortunately there are free resources that may make what can be an overwhelming process much more manageable.

The Florida Department of Children and Families oversees statewide licensing and inspections of child care facilities, specialized childcare facilities for the care of mildly ill children, large family child care homes and licensure or registration of family day care homes. The site provides a Provider Search program that can identify the options, accreditations and programs being sought based on the criteria the user enters.

The options vary from live-in help to enrollment in a group facility, selecting from franchise to independent facilities to hiring an au pair or nanny or having a relative look after youngsters. For helpful ways to evaluate the best options and resources available for your family's particular needs, check out the types of care listed by the Early Learning Coalition of Hillsborough County.

Child Care Resource & Referral is a community service organization that helps parents evaluate, identify, locate and access quality childcare services available locally. A comprehensive list of providers features a wide variety of facilities categorized according to zip code. There's even a checklist with helpful information about what to look for when going through the selection process.

One popular resource for after school programs for children, kindergarteners through fifth graders, are those offered throughout Hillsborough County by the Tampa Metropolitan Area YMCA. Locations vary from public schools to select Y sites.

Tampa…with Tots

With two kids in tow, we're always on the lookout for nearby family-friendly entertainment. In addition to our favorite destinations listed below, we also check out game schedules for the Rays, Buccaneers, and Lightning, as well as shows and concerts at the **Straz Center** and the **Forum**.

Cristin Bishara

Busch Gardens

This sprawling amusement park is a zoo, waterpark (Adventure Island), and roller coaster destination, all rolled into one. Sesame Street of Safari Fun and the Bird Gardens are perfect for our toddler, while our older child enjoys the thrill of the bigger rides. Busch Gardens is open 365 days a year, so we know it's always an entertainment option.

10165 N. McKinley Drive,
www.seaworldparks.com/buschgardens-tampa

Glazer Children's Museum

Perfect for a rainy day, Glazer Children's Museum has seventeen permanent, interactive exhibits, plus a variety of special events. My little one's favorite play areas include KidsPort (a giant water table) and the pretend grocery store. Big sister enjoys creating masterpieces in the Art Lab, as well as climbing Water's Journey, a 35' foot tall structure.

110 W. Gasparilla Plaza

www.glazermuseum.org

Caladesi Island

We love a day at the beach! Only accessible by boat, Caladesi Island is a short ferry ride from Honeymoon Island State Park. Known for its pristine, soft, white sand, the island also has a three-mile nature trail, as well as a kayak route through the mangroves and bay. We try to save time for a stop in nearby quaint, **historic Dunedin** for dinner before heading home.

www.floridastateparks.org/caladesiisland

Lowry Park Zoo

Rated the best zoo in the U.S. by Parents Magazine, Lowry Park is home to more than 1,500 animals, located on 56 acres. With all the usual inhabitants (elephants, zebras, tigers, chimps, and giraffes), our kids enjoy the petting and feeding opportunities, the safari ride, as well as the free-flight aviaries, where exotic birds land on you to eat nectar out of a cup. There are also exhibits that feature Florida animals, such as bobcats, stingrays, and manatees.

1101 W. Sligh Avenue

www.lowryparkzoo.com

The Florida Aquarium

Playful otters and pink roseate spoonbills along the Wetlands Trail are always first on our to-see list. Our kids also love Penguin Point, and during our last visit, we went behind the scenes to pet the penguins. There are daily wild dolphin cruises, and if you're

15 or older, and you are a certified SCUBA diver, you can swim with the aquarium's sharks! Directly behind the aquarium is a small water park, so pack a bathing suit and towel, and an extra change of clothes. Parents can enjoy the cantina bar while their children splash around.

701 Channelside Drive
www.flaquarium.org

MOSI

The Museum of Science and Industry is home to an IMAX* theater, which features stunning documentaries about a variety of natural wonders—great white sharks, butterflies, caves, coral reefs, and Mt. Everest—as well as current box office hits. The MOSI property also includes interactive science exhibits, a butterfly garden, the Saunders Planetarium, and a zip line. Brave, big kids can ride a bike along a wire cable, which is suspended 30 feet above the ground. Our favorite activities at the MOSI are special and seasonal events, such as the annual Festival of Chocolate.

4801 E. Fowler Avenue
www.mosi.org

Dinosaur World

East of Tampa in Plant City, you'll find a massive T. rex waiting to usher you into its prehistoric world. Among the park's lush greenery more than 150 life-sized dinos reside, including Brachiosaurus, Triceratops, Pterodactyl, and Stegosaurus. Kids can play the part of paleontologists and sift through sand searching for fossils. There are two playgrounds, and in the property's museum, you'll discover real dinosaur eggs, raptor claws, and mammoth teeth. Admission rates are quite reasonable, but bring your own picnic lunch, since there are no on-site restaurants.

5145 Harvey Tew Road, Plant City
www.dinosaurworld.com/dinosaur_world_plant_city_florida

Patel Conservatory

Channel your kids' endless creative energy at the Patel Conservatory, a comprehensive arts learning center in downtown Tampa. Part of the Straz Center for the Performing Arts, the Conservatory offers classes for kids pre-K and older. Sign up for ballet, hip-hop, tap, jazz, acting, musical theater, storytelling, violin, vocal arts, or a rock star retreat. Private lessons are available, and summer programs will keep your vacation days filled with artistic fun, too.

1010 North W.C. MacInnes Place
www.patelconservatory.org

CRISTIN BISHARA lives in Tampa with her husband and two girls. She is the author of *Relativity*, a young adult novel published by Bloomsbury.

Public and Private Schools

The Hillsborough County School District consistently ranks among the 10 largest school districts in the country, based on enrollment. Private schools are abundant throughout the county which means parents will have options that can include church-affiliated facilities and non-denominational schools.

A comprehensive list of public and private Hillsborough County schools for children ranging from pre-kindergarten to college and university levels can be one good starting point for getting a feel for the various types and great geographic range of educational facilities available in this community.

Bigger can mean better so be sure to consider what the public school system offers when factoring in your family's educational options.

Noteworthy accomplishments such as leading the state in generating the most National Merit Semifinalists and boasting the nation's second best community college/technical center in the country, Erwin Technical Center, are among some of the standout accomplishments listed among the Hillsborough County School District's "points of pride" in 2013.

Henry B. Plant High School opened in 1927 and is named for railroad and hotel tycoon Henry B. Plant

In addition to more traditional public schools typically offering comprehensive academic missions, Hillsborough County's school system also encompasses magnet schools specializing in theme-based, technology advanced curricula for elementary, middle and high school students. The mix of academics with the selected specialized focus can represent a vigorous, rigorous program that is not necessarily suitable for all students.

For information about enrollment and tuition at private schools, the Tampa Bay Business Journal has compiled a list of 38 schools that reported the largest enrollments as of fall 2013. Tuitions ranged from several thousand dollars per year to just above $20,000 annually.

Many private schools offer pre-kindergarten programs but enrollments may be limited so visiting the campuses to meet with faculty and staff, taking time to observe youngsters in various educational environments and talking to other parents about their experiences is a process that can take time and should be done early enough to meet whatever the enrollment deadline may be.

Want to see how a particular school rates or compares with other comparable educational facilities? There is a rating system for all public schools, from preschools to high schools, as well as private and charter schools located in Hillsborough County.

Tampa Public or Charter Schools
Top Ranking from 8 to 10 out of 10

Elementary

- Bryant Elementary School
- Chiles Elementary School
- Coleman Middle School
- Gorrie Elementary School
- Mabry Elementary School
- Mitchell Elementary School

Middle Schools

- Coleman Middle School
- Williams Middle Magnet School
- Wilson Middle School
- Farnell Middle School
- Channelside Academy Middle School
- Benito Middle School

High Schools

- Plant High School
- Brooks Debartolo Collegiate High School
- Sickles High School
- Newsome High School
- Winegrass Ranch High School
- Steinbrenner High School

Source: GreatSchools.org

After School Educational Activities

Whether you are seeking after school activities including ways to cultivate children's creative tendencies beyond the classroom or just want to work more athletic endeavors into their weekly schedules, there are plenty of resources exist to address those needs.

For a more creative approach to learning, above and beyond the traditional pillars of reading, writing and arithmetic, families may choose from a wide variety of performing arts training programs offered through the Patel Conservatory, a facility affiliated with the David A. Straz Jr., Center for the Performing Arts. The three-story, 45,000-square-foot center offers more than 100 classes in dance, theater and music for children, ages 2 and up. The schedule presents an entertaining mix of classes and summer camp programs that can help develop skills in a child that will serve them well throughout life. The kids don't get to have all of the fun. There are classes open to adults as well.

Have a future gymnast in the family or someone who thinks they can dance? The Tampa Parks and Recreation Department coordinates competitive and recreational gymnastics and dance programs for energetic youths ages 1 - 17.

For those who want sports activities beyond those available through individual schools, please note that Hillsborough County is a hub for youth sports leagues. Offerings include baseball, cheerleading, football, flag football, soccer and softball leagues. Make your picks from youth sports programs offered at 59 publicly owned athletic facilities countywide.

A franchise youth sports league based in Tampa offers leagues, camps and clinics for boys and girls ages 3 - 17. The fastest growing youth sports organization of its kind in the U.S., i9 Sports provides a full schedule of popular sports for children of all levels and so they can participate without tryouts or drafts, focusing more on the fun and camaraderie of team sports rather than keeping score and being fiercely competitive.

Day camps and specialty camps offered through the Hillsborough County Parks, Recreation and Conservation Department are also available June - August for youngsters ages 5 - 17 as well as for special needs participants ages 5 - 22. Fees vary according to the camp, ranging from day rates to multi-week enrollments, and income-based discounts are available.

Many of the area's attractions, arts facilities and even retail centers are increasingly creating fun ways for youngsters to spend their school breaks. Those can range from photography classes and cooking lessons to learning how to make movies and even enjoying animal encounters offered by Lowry

Lowry Park Zoo is one of the local attractions that offers special programs for children during the summer months. Photo courtesy of Dave Parkinson

Park Zoo and AquaCamp aquatic adventures available at the Florida Aquarium. Check with individual museums, organizations like the Tampa YMCA or media outlets like Tampa Bay Parenting Magazine for calendars and schedules.

Higher Education: College and Beyond

Whether you are interested in pursuing a four-year degree, learning a new trade or staying competitive in your field by furthering your education, you can make that, and more, happen here. Major universities, colleges, trade and technical schools as well as graduate schools and highly regarded law, medical and MBA programs serve students of all ages and all nationalities.

University of South Florida

The University of South Florida (USF) is based right here in Tampa, despite what its name might imply. The main Tampa campus is joined by two other West Coast accredited institutions, USF St. Petersburg and USF Sarasota-Manatee. With an enrollment topping 47,000 students, USF ranks as one of the largest public universities in the U.S.

The history of USF is filled with groundbreaking achievements that have furthered its educational mission and enhanced its reputation as a global research university. Highlights of its milestones and major accomplishments are too lengthy to list here but can be reviewed on a web page appropriately named "Points of Pride."

USF has come a long way from its infancy as a commuter school with no high profile sports programs and little more than basic educational offerings to draw students to campus. Currently there are more than 600 recognized student organizations affiliated with the North Tampa campus. Not only is there student housing but there is a selection of living spaces, ranging from traditional college dorms to suite-style halls to apartments complete with kitchens.

Founded in 1956, USF was at that time aptly named since it was the southernmost university in Florida as well as the state's first metropolitan university. When its first classes convened Set. 26, 1960, USF became the first major state university planned, built and opened in the 20th century.

There are 17 men's and women's varsity teams competing in NCAA divisions but the one thing that USF lacks that still differentiates it from some of its collegiate colleagues is an on-campus football stadium. The USF Bulls football team competes at Raymond James Stadium whenever they host games.

The Tampa campus is home to USF Health, comprised of its Colleges of Medicine, Nursing, Public Health and Pharmacy. From the comparatively humble beginnings of a community medical school established in 1965, USF has emerged a major medical center. The Morsani College of Medicine is an aggressive, progressive college that is home of one of the world's largest freestanding Alzheimer's centers and the USF Diabetes Center, which is at the forefront of diabetes and autoimmune treatment and research.

In 2012. USF established the first-of-its-kind, 90,000-square-foot Center for Advanced Medical Learning and Simulation (CAMlS) in downtown Tampa, a $38 million facility that provides training in the most advanced surgical techniques using robotics and other state-of-the-art medical devices. The impact of USF goes beyond the number of degrees it bestows on students. It is an economic generator that brings jobs to this community and provides an impact that goes far beyond the county lines.

University of Tampa

One of the area's most distinctive institutions of higher learning is also a local landmark.

The University of Tampa (UT) is readily recognizable for its Moorish and Turkish architecture and distinctive minarets, domes and cupolas that are part of the downtown Tampa landscape.

Originally built as a lavish winter resort that opened in 1891, the former 511-room Tampa Bay Hotel is now a National Historic Landmark as well as home to UT and the Henry B. Plant Museum.

The seasonal hotel remained open until 1932 when it was called into military service and used as an encampment by Colonel Teddy Roosevelt and his Rough Riders during the Spanish-American War. The hotel heirs eventually sold the grand building to the City of Tampa in 1905. What began as the Tampa Junior College in 1931 transformed into UT two years later. Today the former ritzy hotel rooms are used for offices and classes while only one wing of Plant Hall has been preserved as the Henry B. Plant Museum.

It would be 20 years before the college was accredited but its current achievements and accomplishments continue to draw praise and high marks from the likes of The Princeton Review and U.S. News & World Report particularly for UT's Sykes Business College.

The picturesque, private, co-educational university serves more than 7,200 undergraduate and graduate students from across the U.S. and from around the world and has grown to occupy more than 100-acres offering a lovely, riverfront setting for its 58-building campus. While it may seem students are drawn here for the Florida weather and casual lifestyle, UT is home to serious scholarship. UT's top 10 undergraduate majors are: international business, biology, psychology, management, nursing, marine science, sport management, communication, criminology and finance.

This historic campus' proximity to downtown's business sector and cultural hub has been a boon to students seeking internships or volunteer opportunities that can enhance their opportunities for future, full time employment.

The university's NCAA Division II team rosters include a lively mix of sports for both men and women, including cross-country, golf, lacrosse, swimming, soccer, basketball and track. In addition crew, softball, tennis and volleyball are available to women and baseball for men.

Stetson University College of Law

The Tampa Law Center of Stetson University College of Law owes its existence to a public-private partnership, the first venture of its kind in Florida. The three-story Mediterranean-style building located on the outskirts of downtown Tampa is home to the Tampa branch of Florida's Second District Court of Appeal as well as a satellite campus offering evening classes. Founded in 1900 as Florida's first law school, Stetson moved from DeLand to Gulfport, a small community adjacent to St. Petersburg, in 1954.

Among Stetson's noteworthy accomplishments are top marks received from U.S. News & World Report for trial advocacy and legal writing and its distinction as the first Florida law school to require pro bono service by students and faculty.

The Tampa campus of Stetson University College of Law

Hillsborough Community College

Hillsborough Community College (HCC) serves students at five primary locations through distance learning programs, and the Institute for Corporate and Continuing Education (ICCE). Class enrollments are relatively small by design to encourage interaction between students and faculty members. Founded in 1968, HCC offers courses for students seeking associate degrees in business-related fields, technical programs, health science programs, college credit certificates and postsecondary adult vocational programs.

The Dale Mabry campus, located near Raymond James Stadium, also boasts an invigorating array of student athletic programs that include baseball, basketball, softball, tennis and volleyball.

Art Institute of Tampa

The Art Institute of Tampa offers students a variety of ways to learn and earn associate degrees as well as diplomas and certificate programs specializing in design, media arts, fashion and the culinary arts. Established in 2004, it is a branch of he Miami International University of Art & Design and among more than 45 similar educational institutions found throughout North America.

The culinary program gives students real world experience at running an on-site restaurant, The Tutored Chef. They create the menu, make the meals and serve the freshly prepared dishes. Diners can even observe the kitchen crew through a large window. Hours and days of operation are limited but the restaurant is open to the public, providing a delicious dining experience for a fraction of the price that would be charged at a for-profit eating establishment.

CHAPTER 7

OUR DIVERSIFIED ECONOMY

Doing Business in Tampa

Maybe there's something in the water that made Bass Pro Shops want to cast its line Tampa's way and expand to Brandon.

Maybe there's something in the air that convinced Copa Airlines to begin nonstop service from Tampa to its Panama City hub and Edelweiss Air to launch long distance hauls whisking passengers from Tampa to Zurich.

Passengers arrive and depart from Tampa International Airport for business as well as leisure travel.

Or, maybe there's just something about Tampa's well-educated, multi-lingual workforce, on-going population growth, central location and commercial shipping system that convinces major decision makers to wake up, smell the Cuban coffee and realize Tampa is very good for business.

Whatever "it" is, it's working and that means more work for more people. Tampa has a relatively strong job market in comparison to other areas of the country and its multi-faceted economy has helped the area continue to not just survive but thrive.

As of November 2013, the Tampa-St. Petersburg-Clearwater metropolitan statistical area (MRSA) had a 6.2% unemployment rate, which compares favorably with the national average of 6.6%, according to the U.S. Department of Labor.

Tampa boasts a robust hospitality industry fueled by a major theme park and a major employer in Busch Gardens, outstanding convention, trade show and conference facilities, a popular airport, a vibrant cruise ship industry and an impressive array of amateur and professional sports venues. But, don't make the mistake of thinking that Tampa is just about sun and fun.

The cruise ship Legend departs from Tampa's deep-water port.

In fact, the Tampa Hillsborough Economic Development Corp. (EDC) notes that this area is home to more than 19 corporate headquarters each generating more than $1 billion in annual revenues. Healthcare and medical technology, international trade and finance are among Tampa's major industries that are expected to keep going and growing in the years ahead.

As a designated foreign trade zone, our city can eliminate import duties from being charged on goods shipped to Tampa designated for repacking, storage or transshipment. And when it comes to moving goods, Tampa benefits from the commercial shipping facilities offered by Tampa International Airport, the CSX railway system, a network of nearby interstate and state highways and the Port Tampa Bay, the largest cargo port in Florida.

Tampa International Airport consistently ranks among the leading airports worldwide.

Innovation and technology are increasingly becoming a focal point of future local growth. The Tampa Bay area is among 23 counties collectively known as the Florida High Tech Corridor, an economic development initiative that comprises high tech companies, research institutions and industry organizations.

Tampa is also home to MacDill Air Force Base, the global headquarters of U.S. Central Command and U.S. Special Operations

MacDill Air Force Base is a vital link to global military operations.

In addition, Hillsborough County's legacy as an agricultural leader for Florida continues to rank it among the leading producers in the state.

And there's much more to come in the months and years ahead.

Highlights of what's ahead and happening include:

USAA, a financial services company, plans to add up to 1,215 jobs by 2019 when a new 420,000-square-foot, $164 million facility opens in Brandon

HealthPlan Services, headquartered in Tampa, plans to expand by 1,000 jobs over the next few years

Amazon is building distribution centers in Ruskin, located east of Tampa, and Lakeland, which is between Tampa and Orlando, which will collectively add about 1,000 jobs.

Bristol-Myers Squibb, a global biopharmaceutical firm, opened a North America Capability Center near Tampa International Airport in 2014 that added nearly 600 jobs by 2017

James Hardie, a global Ireland-based manufacturer of fiber cement siding, plans to invest $80 million to expand its Plant City operations and create 100 new jobs by 2015.

The Tampa Bay Partnership compiles information about the leading industries and employers within a multi-county area encompassing Hillsborough, Pinellas, Polk, Pasco, Citrus, Sarasota and Manatee counties. Collectively, the 50 public and private companies listed each employed more than 1,000 people in 2013.

The Greater Tampa Chamber of Commerce characterizes the current business climate as follows:

"We boast a diverse and expanding mix of businesses, from financial services and bioscience, to technology and international trade. As the economy begins to kick back into gear, the Tampa Bay region is looking to a bright future of continued job creation. This will be particularly true of the industry clusters that make Tampa the gateway to Florida's High Tech Corridor including life sciences, nanotechnology, aviation/ aerospace and homeland security/defense."

Tampa Bay Economic Climate

With a cost of living well below the national average, a mild seasonal climate and a robust assortment of cultural and recreational amenities, it's no surprise that Tampa Bay is a top destination for residents and visitors alike.

We enjoy access to world-class health care, an exceptional education system at every level of learning, and neighborhoods as diverse as the landscape itself. Rivers, lakes and nearby beaches, along with the eponymous Tampa Bay, offer ample opportunities for year-round outdoor adventures, with thousands of acres of parks and trails for hiking, biking and exploring the natural beauty of Florida.

The region is home to four professional sports teams, the spring training destination of six Major League Baseball teams, and a frequent host of world-class athletic events, from the Super Bowl to the PGA Tour. Here you'll find an expansive collection of award-winning museums and attractions, along with some of the top entertainment venues in the country and an annual roster of festivals and events that contribute to a growing list of exciting local discoveries.

We are one of the best places in America to do business, offering affordability, accessibility and an unwavering commitment to corporate success.

We drive innovation and technology in medicine, manufacturing, agriculture and defense, and are widely regarded as one of the premiere financial services centers in the country. Here, you'll find a competitive environment with room to grow and resources to thrive, as well as an abundance of exceptional economic assets, including the Port Tampa Bay, Tampa International Airport, the University of South Florida and MacDill Air Force Base.

By air, land or sea, we provide the critical connectivity you need to succeed in the continuous cycle of global business activity.

Tampa International Airport (TPA) offers non-stop flights to over 70 domestic and international destinations, with recent route expansions adding direct access to Switzerland and Panama. Serving approximately 17 million people each year, TPA ranks among the top North American aviation facilities and is the only U.S. location to be named one of the 10 "most-loved" airports in the world.

The 5,000-acre Port Tampa Bay is the largest and most diverse seaport in Florida. One of the country's premiere shipbuilding and repair centers, the Port of Tampa is also the nation's closest deep-water gateway to the Panama Canal, providing unparalleled access to Latin American markets. Interstates 4, 75 and 275 also link the region to 30 million consumers in major U.S. cities, all within an eight-hour drive.

We deliver an exceptional workforce trained in the skills companies need today, as we prepare our students for the jobs of tomorrow.

The Tampa metro area is one of the Top 20 markets in the country, and the population center of the eight-county region. More than 4.2 million residents and an active labor force of nearly 2 million ensure an abundance of qualified candidates to fulfill employer demand.

Florida has the top talent pipeline in the country, bolstered by a state college and university system that introduces over 165,000 new graduates to the workforce each year. Tampa Bay is home to nearly 80 colleges, universities and technical schools, including the University of South Florida (USF), one of the country's largest public universities with more than 47,000 students. USF is also one of the Top 50 elite research institutions in the nation and ranked 10th worldwide in the number of U.S. patents granted.

Our companies enjoy low labor costs, favorable tax policies, no personal income tax and stable, pro-business leadership.

Locally, collaboration between government and industry has resulted in effective development practices, expedited permitting and a streamlined regulatory process, reinforcing the annual accolades that recognize the area as an ideal place to start, grow and succeed in business.

Currently, the Tampa metropolitan area leads the state of Florida in job gains. In the past two years alone, more than 50 companies have selected Hillsborough County as the site of their relocation and expansion activities, generating over 8,700 new jobs and $688 million in capital investment. Global market leaders, including Bristol-Myers Squibb, Morgan Stanley, The Depository Trust & Clearing Corporation, Time Warner Business Services, USAA and Amazon have expressed their confidence in our community by announcing plans for significant, strategic growth.

In Hillsborough County and the cities of Tampa, Plant City and Temple Terrace, our brightest days are yet to come. In this exciting new era of growth and prosperity, your potential is limited only by your imagination.

So think big, we do.

RICK HOMANS
President and CEO
Tampa Hillsborough Economic
Development Corporation

Rick Homans

CHAPTER 8
FITTING IN AND FINDING OUT

Like most Southern cities, Tampa knows how to be hospitable. But newcomers may find it takes a little time, and effort, to feel really at home here.

Growing up locally has its advantages in terms of getting to know some of the more well-established families who have called Tampa home for generations and whose names are immortalized on city street signs, public schools and even high-rise office buildings.

Breaking into those circles may seem a bit daunting at first, but there are many ways to connect with community leaders and power brokers.

Finding common bonds, discovering mutual friends or getting to know those seated around you at Tampa Opera, during Tampa Bay Buccaneer football games or while enjoying Florida Orchestra concerts, can help you quickly create a new network of personal and professional contacts.

No matter when you graduated from college or how long it has been since you set foot on your university campus, check with your alma mater, or do an online search, to locate where and when alumni organizations may be gathering locally.

Who you know can be helpful in terms of getting a fast pass into some of the more exclusive golf and country clubs, membership-based organizations and long-established social groups like Ye Mystic Krewe of Gasparilla, whose male members participate in numerous community and charity events but who also help put on Tampa's annual all-day, pirate-themed invasion and parade, Gasparilla.

Volunteer Opportunities

Find a cause you want to support and you are likely to find not only how to make a difference but also a great way to make new friends.

Volunteering is an ideal way to combine your particular passion with discovering other like-minded individuals. Government agencies, community organizations and major events may provide excellent opportunities to get to meet people while also providing a helping hand.

Love helping animals? You can help wash and groom rescues, foster them at your home or provide social contact to help calm a fearful animal by taking it for a walk. Hillsborough County's Animal Services provides a list of volunteers activities and ways to help.

Metropolitan Ministries supports poor and homeless families from a four-county area. Volunteers are vital to the organization, especially during times when large donations of food are dropped off, or during holidays, like Thanksgiving, when extra help is needed preparing and serving meals. But there are on-going volunteer needs throughout the year as well.

Keep Tampa Bay Beautiful organizes community clean-ups, beautification and restoration projects that can be beneficial, and fun, for all ages. Annual events include the Great American Cleanup in April and the Hillsborough River & Coastal Cleanup each September.

Arts and cultural events and programs rely heavily on volunteers for a variety of tasks that can range from marketing assistance, staffing information tables or helping with anything from set-building for stage productions to ushering at performances. For a sample of those arts-related opportunities, check out the Volunteers Needed section of the Hillsborough County Arts Council website.

High profile groups and organizations with local chapters or offices include Habitat for Humanity, an organization that helps first-time homebuyers and families access affordable housing. Big Brothers Big Sisters of Tampa Bay welcomes volunteers of all ages, and from all walks of life, who want to provide friendship, support and stability to help make a difference in the life of a child.

Major fundraising events crowd the social calendars of lots of residents throughout the year. These can be excellent events that allow you to get involved and get acquainted for the cost of a ticket or the price for a place at the table.

Some are celebrity-studded like the DeBartolo Family Foundation All Star Charity Gala that features famous athletes, musicians and chefs. Its mission is to "provide leadership and financial resources to extraordinary organizations and individuals to improve the community."

The Magnolia Ball is another top-tier, fundraising event that benefits the H. Lee Moffitt Cancer Center. This yearly event has raised millions of dollars for patient care, research and education.

Pavilion, Tampa Museum of Art's premier black tie event, provides funding for exhibitions and educational programs presented by the museum.

Pavilion at Tampa Museum of Art

115

If getting gussied up for a gala isn't your thing, there's always the Cattle Barons' Ball that benefits the American Cancer Society. Think boots, Stetsons, and big belt buckles rather than tuxedos and evening gowns.

Or look into local golf tournaments, running or walking events or other engaging ways to support a cause and be part of a group, like the Miles for Moffitt races held at the University of South Florida that raises money for research programs.

Miles for Moffitt annual racing event held at the University of South Florida

The Tampa Bay Times tackles the monumental task of creating a society datebook each year that can help ensure you keep all of these important dates straight. It's a comprehensive list of what's happening and who's entertaining at these high profile soirees.

After all of the fundraising, maybe you just need time for some fun.

There are plenty of ways to enjoy all types of activities that can even more enjoyable with others. Meet up groups can provide fun ways to explore the area while also meeting new people. Or sharing common ground, like an interest in environmental concerns or ecological issues, could be a great motivation for checking out the Sierra Club Tampa Bay or the Tampa Audubon Society.

Of course, one of the easiest ways to come in contact with others may be during your daily or weekly routines, whether they take you to your children's school, the church, temple or place of worship of your choice, the dog park or the neighborhood community center.

Local Media

The multi-county area that includes Hillsborough and Pinellas counties ranks among the Top 20 media markets nationwide. In addition, the Tampa Bay area remains one of the few remaining markets served by two daily newspapers in the U.S.

Tampa Bay's culturally and demographically diverse population is reflected in the print, broadcast and online media outlets available here. There are radio and TV formats for Spanish-speaking audiences, publications that focus on families or specialize in topics of interest to seniors and outlets targeting members of LGBT (lesbian, gay, bisexual and transgender) communities. Regional magazines published locally focus on fashion, dining, entertainment, high-end real estate and lifestyle topics.

La Gaceta Newspaper **is a weekly publication that features three languages, English, Spanish and Italian**

The market's two daily newspapers are the _Tampa Tribune_ and the _Tampa Bay Times_. The *Tampa Bay Times* also publishes a free Monday-Friday paper called TBT that covers current events along with entertainment, food, fashion, sports and celebrity news.

Business Publications

Florida Trend Magazine is a monthly statewide publication with articles about about business leaders, major industries and issues that affect companies of all types and sizes. Articles about trends, forecasts, research and development, industries from agriculture to technology plus profiles of past, present, and possibly future, business leaders are among its main topics.

Tampa Bay Business Journal is a weekly publication specializing in local business news in commercial real estate, banking and finance, retail and restaurant, health care and all types of professions from architecture and advertising to transportation and the law.

Bi-Weekly & Weekly Publications

Centro Tampa is a free Spanish language tabloid published by the Tampa Tribune.

Creative Loafing is a free publication focused on local politics, music, arts, entertainment, dining, the creative arts and social issues.

La Gaceta, the only tri-lingual newspaper in the U.S., prints articles about politics, local and international news, events and more in English, Spanish and Italian.

Florida Sentinel Bulletin is a bi-weekly publication featuring local news and news of interest to the African-American community.

Lifestyle Magazines

Bay Magazine is a luxury, lifestyle magazine published and distributed by the Tampa Bay Times.

DuPont Registry is a regional publication that features upscale homes, fashion trends, new products and upcoming entertainment, from Broadway touring productions to exhibits opening at art museums.

Edible Tampa Bay focuses on local businesses, local food sources, restaurants featuring farm-to-fork menus and other locally based enterprises ranging from the craft beer breweries to the independent markets and farmers' markets found in Tampa Bay.

South Tampa Magazine highlights businesses like fitness clubs, centers specializing in cosmetic treatments, local restaurants and bars and hair salons.

Tampa Bay Metro offers a comprehensive overview of what is happening in the community, from fundraising events and annual black tie galas to new restaurants, where to find the latest fashions and overviews of what is available locally from top medical facilities to the leading private schools.

Tampa Bay covers the arts, special events, restaurants, travel destinations and profiles of local personalities.

Lifestyles After 50 specializes in news about events, activities and programs of interest to the 50-plus crowd.

Parent Guide is resource for family friendly events and activities and items of interest to anyone raising young children.

Tampa Bay Parenting is a resource for family friendly events and activities and items of interest to anyone raising young children.

Watermark Magazine specializes in subjects of interest to members of the lesbian, gay, bisexual or transgender communities ranging from legal issues to upcoming elections, to local reviews and events plus information about new businesses and legislative topics.

Local TV Stations

The Tampa Bay area is the nation's 14th-largest TV market, according to Nielsen Media Research,[4] reaching 1.78 million TV households.

WEDU (Channel 3, PBS)
WFLA (Channel 8, NBC)
WTSP (Channel 10, CBS)
WTVT (Channel 13, Fox)
WUSF (Channel 16, PBS)
WFTS (Channel 28, ABC)

WMOR (Channel 32, Ind.)
WTOG (Channel 44, The CW)
WRMD (Channel 49, Telemundo)
WFTT(Channel 50, Unimas 50)
WVEA (Channel 62, Univision)

Local cable-only stations include Bay News 9 and Bright House Sports Network (operated by Bright House Networks).

InfoMás is Tampa and Orlando's first regional network offering around-the-clock news and information all in Spanish. Channel 900 – and channel 1211 and channel 1900 for InfoMás HD – offer local, national and international news along with weather, sports and special features including medical reports, political coverage and entertainment news.

A half-hour magazine program, Revista InfoMás, covers news subjects such as political issues, immigration, school issues and other matters that affect the local Hispanic community. Revista InfoMás airs Monday through Friday at 11 a.m.

Source: www.stationindex.com/tv/markets/Tampa-St.+Petersburg

Radio
Local Radio Stations - FM

WMNF- 88.5 (Non-commercial community radio/music/news/ public affairs)
WYFE - 88.9 (Religious)
WMTX - 89.3 (Adult contemporary)
WUSF - 89.7 (News/music/educational public radio)
WBVM - 90.5 (Christian contemporary)
WFTI - 91.7 (Christian contemporary)
WYUU - 92.5 (Spanish)
WFLZ - 93.3 (Top 40)
WWRM - 94.9 (Adult contemporary)
WDAE - 95.3 (Sports)
WBTP - 95.7 (Hip hop)
WVVD - 96.5 (Spanish)

WFLA - 96.7 (News/talk)
WSUN - 97.1 (Alternative)
WXTB - 97.9 (Rock)
WQYK - 99.5 (Country)
WMTX - 100.7 (Adult contemporary)
WPOI - 101.5 (Top 40)
WFUS - 103.5 (Country)
WRBQ - 104.7 (Classic hits)
WDUV - 105.5 (Easy listening)
WXGL - 107.3 (Classic hits)

Local Radio Stations - AM

WTBN - 570 (Religious)
WGES - 680 (Spanish)
WLCC - 760 (Spanish)
WWBA - 820 (News/talk)
WGUL - 860 (Talk)
WTWD - 910 (Religious)
WFLA - 970 (News/talk)
WHFS - 1010 (Sports)
WHBO - 1040 (Sports)
WTIS - 1110 (Religious)
WTMP - 1150 (Spanish)
WHNZ - 1250 (Talk)
WQBN - 1300 (Spanish)
WTAN - 1340 (Talk)
WWMI - 1380 (Children's)
WMGG - 1470 (Talk)
WAMA -1550 (Regional Mexican)
WXRB - 1590 (Gospel music)

www.radio-locator.com/cgi-bin/locate?select=city&city=Tampa

CHAPTER 9
ON THE MOVE TO TAMPA

People - and their belongings - are really on the move in the Tampa Bay area.

An analytical report released in 2014 by the Penske Truck Rental Company revealed that only Atlanta out-scored this area for one-way consumer truck rental reservations.

One caveat is attached to that conclusion. The survey included Sarasota in its Tampa Bay findings which may have helped boost Tampa's standing in the rankings.

Of course, not everyone necessarily uses Penske trucks. Another moving company that is headquartered in Tampa is College Hunks Moving that offers local, statewide and limited interstate moving options. They can pack, load, move and remove whatever you need them to tackle.

The professional moving firm has partnered with another Tampa Bay-based company that offers on-site storage. PODS provides portable storage facilities that can safely and securely keep your personal belongings on your property while your new home is being built or renovations are being completed.

That means 12-foot or 16-foot portable storage containers can be delivered directly to your location for short- or long-term storage. And, with the help of College Hunks Moving, loading or unloading these containers can be part of the deal.

Getting references and referrals for movers can be very helpful. One resource for finding reputable moving companies can be through the Better Business Bureau. Another good place to learn more about professional moving companies is the American Moving & Storage Association.

For guidelines that can help to ensure your move goes smoothly, review the "Choose the Right Moving Company" tips listed on USA. gov.

If may be helpful to do some online research to find reviews, ratings and helpful tips from others who have previously gone through the moving process. Angie's List has posted a comprehensive list of ways to prepare and plan, how to hire a moving company, common mistakes that are made and ways to estimate an approximate cost.

CONCLUSION

Welcome to Tampa, a great city that continues to thrive, thrill, surprise, delight and exceed all expectations.

Great cities are both love-able and live-able. They exude excitement and energy. They are dynamic and diverse. They are appealing and affordable. And they enable people to find their own place within the community once they find their way there.

While Tampa benefits from its central location within one of the nation's most highly populated states, it's a city that has always made its own way, created its own destiny and managed to take charge and make change for the better.

There is a lot to like here already but there is additional untapped potential as well as the city continues to develop. It's no wonder multi-national companies, major league sports, international flights, world-class medical facilities and entrepreneurial ventures are all part of the Tampa vibe.

It's always been difficult to define exactly what Tampa is simply because it doesn't fit neatly into any one niche. But it is that ability to be many things to many people that has served this city well, helping it to to weather economic downturns, remain resilient while other areas suffered and successfully rebound from any setbacks, whether natural or manmade.

Take a look around Tampa and get a glimpse of its future. Look in any direction and you'll easily spot major roads that are being built, commercial construction projects rising from the ground and new residential developments under way.

Talk to the residents, business owners and community leaders. Walk along its sidewalks and wade along its waterfront. Enjoy a cafe con leche, a made-in-Tampa micro-brewed beer, a salad created from locally sourced, organic greens or just-caught fresh seafood.

One you get a feel for the city, and a taste for Tampa, you may decide that this is the place you need to be.

VALUABLE RESOURCES AND SOURCES OF INFORMATION

Local, County, State and Federal Government Agencies

City of Tampa
www.tampagov.net
(813)274-8211

Guide to City Services
www.tampagov.net/files/city_services_guide.pdf

City of Tampa Utilities
www.tampagov.net/dept_city_of_tampa_utilities
(813) 274-8811

City of Plant City
www.plantcitygov.com
(813) 659-4200

City of Temple Terrace
www.templeterrace.com
(813) 506-6420

Hillsborough County Government
www.hillsboroughcounty.org
(813)272-5900

Hillsborough County Clerk of the Circuit Court
www.hillsclerk.com/publicweb/marriage_faq.aspx
(813)276-8100

Hillsborough County Emergency Management/
Tampa Bay Regional Planning Council
www.tampabayprepares.org
(727) 570-5151

Hillsborough County Property Appraiser
www.hcpafl.org
(813)272-6100

Hillsborough County Public Schools
www.sdhc.k12.fl.us
(813) 272-4000

Hillsborough County Supervisor of Elections
www.votehillsborough.org
(813)272-5850 (813) 744-5900

Hillsborough County Tax Collector
www.hillstax.org
(813)635-5200

Florida Department of Highway Safety and Motor Vehicles/
Hillsborough County Service Centers
www.flhsmv.gov/offices/hillsborough.html
(850)617-2000

Tampa Florida Social Security Office
www.socialsecurityofficelocation.net/tampa-florida-social-security-office-so1627
(800)772-1213

Major Medical Facilities

Tampa General Hospital
www.tgh.org
(813) 844-7000

St. Joseph's Hospital BayCare Health System
www.sjbhealth.org/homepage.cfm?id=584&gclid=CKC-qMCGt-boCFWho7AodTBUAEw
(813_ 870-4000

Tampa Shriners Hospital for Children
www.sahibshrine.org/hospitals
(813) 972-2250

H. Lee Moffitt Cancer Center & Research Institute
www.moffitt.org
(813) 745-4673

Public Transportation

HART (Hillsborough Area Regional Transit Authority)
www.gohart.org
(813) 254-4278

TECO Line Streetcar System
www.tecolinestreetcar.org
(813) 254-4278

Tampa International Airport
www.tampaairport.com
(813) 870-8700

Tampa Port Authority Cruise Terminals
www.tampaport.com/cruise.aspx
(813) 905-7678

AMTRAK
www.amtrak.com/servlet/ContentServer?pagename=am/am2Station/
Station_Page&code=TPA
(800) 872-7245

Economic Development

Tampa Hillsborough Economic Development Corp.
www.tampaedc.com
(813) 218-3300

Tampa Bay Partnership
www.tampabay.org
(800) 556-9316

Tampa Bay Technology Forum
www.tbtf.org
(813) 341-8283

Hillsborough County Economic Development Initiative
www.hillsboroughcounty.org/index.aspx?NID=3109
(813) 272-6217

Hillsborough County Small/Minority Business Development
www.hillsboroughcounty.org/index.aspx?nid=335
(813) 914-4028

Small Business Development Center at the
University of South Florida
www.sbdctampabay.com
(813) 905-5800

Tampa/Hillsborough County Statistical Information
www.city-data.com/city/Tampa-Florida.html

Greater Tampa Chamber of Commerce
www.tampachamber.com
(813) 228-7777

Law Enforcement

Tampa Police Department
www.tampagov.net/dept_police
Emergencies: 911
Non-Emergencies: (813) 231-6130

Hillsborough County Sheriff's Department
www.hcso.tampa.fl.us/
Emergencies: 911
Non-Emergencies: (813) 247-8200

Utilities

Tampa Electric Co.
www.tampaelectric.com
Hillsborough County (813) 223-0800

Peoples Gas
www.peoplesgas.com
Tampa (813) 275-3700 or
1-877 TECO PGS (1-877-832-6747) TOLL FREE

Central Florida Gas
www.fpuc.com/centralfloridagasinfo
(800) 427-7712

City of Tampa Water Department
www.tampagov.net/dept_water/index.asp
(813) 274-8121

Moving to Tampa: The Un-Tourist Guide Website

For the most up-to-date information about making the Tampa area your new home, visit the companion web site to this book: www.MovingtoTampaGuide.com

For lists and hyperlink access to the online resources, go to: www.MovingtoTampaGuide.com/resources

ACKNOWLEDGEMENTS

Newt Barrett is the visionary who created this series and the incredibly patient and understanding person who dealt with many delays and countless questions from me.

So many of the beautiful photographs found on the cover and throughout the pages were created and graciously provided by Gerardo Luna, a true talent with a camera, a genuinely positive individual and a tireless worker at whatever he does, from photography to real estate.

A great big thank you to the following organizations who contributed photos that help bring Tampa to life for our readers. Your pictures really make our book more readable and enjoyable.

- Baker Barrios Architects
- Columbia Restaurant
- International Plaza
- Lowry Park Zoo
- Moffitt Cancer Center
- Outback Bowl
- Oxford Exchange
- Straz Performing Arts Center
- Tampa General Hospital
- Tampa International Airport
- Tampa Museum of Art
- Tampa Port Authority
- U.S. Air Force
- Visit Tampa Bay

All of the columnists were incredibly generous of their time, their passion for their hometown and their invaluable insights. Thank you to the tireless Richard Gonzmart, stylish Nancy Vaughn, tasteful Mary Scourtes, gifted Gerardo Luna, uber-marketer Rick Homans and multi-talented Maddy Krasne.

A project like this is a big undertaking and I must thank friend, associate and fellow author of the *Moving To St. Petersburg* book, Cindy Dobyns for her on-going encouragement.

And because this is my first - and likely my only book - thanks to my loving parents, Russ and Barbara Janson. I owe them a heartfelt thanks for the opportunity to grow up in Tampa from age 10.

My lifelong love affair with journalism began at Tampa's Henry B. Plant High School where I was editor of the yearbook my senior year. A former neighbor encouraged me to enroll in Journalism 101 at the University of Florida. Paul Hogan was not only a neighbor but managing editor of the *Tampa Tribune* at that time and when I came home for Christmas and summer vacations, he hired me to work part time at the newspaper.

The faculty at the University of Florida taught me well, worked me hard and prepared me for what some may call a job but I consider a lifetime of learning and a lifelong passion.

I will never forget the first morning I woke up, picked up the *Tampa Tribune* newspaper and saw my byline printed on the page. I still get that same thrill whether writing for *Tampa Bay Metro Magazine, Edible Tampa Bay, DuPont Registry Magazine* or for VisitSouth.com.

Thanks to all who have been part of this journey and this project.

ABOUT THE AUTHOR

It was chance that first brought Mary Lou Janson to the Tampa Bay area - Tampa specifically - but choice that has made it her home far longer than anywhere else she has lived.

A family vacation that combined visiting relatives with an escape from the frigid February weather in Canton, OH, her former hometown, first introduced Mary Lou to the natural beauty and better weather this Central Florida city boasts.

It was a traumatic move for a then 10-year-old to be uprooted from friends and relatives and transplanted to the Tampa Hyde Park neighborhood that became her new home.

She remained in Tampa and other areas of Florida until making the cross-country leap to Berkeley, CA to live on the other West Coast in the 90s. It was a wonderful five-year stay but by then the "boomerang effect" took hold. That is the nickname she has for the Tampa phenomenon defined by longtime residents leaving but eventually returning to reclaim their Tampa roots.

A writer and publicist, her journalism career spans more than 30 years. A former *Tampa Tribune* reporter, she covered Florida's tourism and agricultural industries as well as issues related directly to the Tampa Bay area.

When named the public relations manager of the primary destination marketing organization for Tampa/Hillsborough County, she worked with journalists from around the world to introduce them to what makes Tampa a popular travel destination. During that time, she received a national award for the comprehensive press kit she researched, wrote and developed to promote and publicize what Tampa offers travelers who come here for fun, to visit friends and family or for business purposes.

Most of her life has been spent in the Tampa Bay area, where she currently lives, works and enjoys the natural beauty, signature sunsets and warm weather on almost a daily basis. She continues to share her favorite things about Tampa with others via her blog on VisitSouth. com, the app she created for Sutro Media, the Insider's Guide to Tampa Bay, and through articles in local magazines like *Tampa Bay Metro, DuPont Registry* and *Edible Tampa Bay.*

Tampa is an area that continues to evolve and expand an endless source of delightful discoveries.

Mary Lou hopes to help others will feel at home here as much as she does.

20293845R10077

Made in the USA
Middletown, DE
21 May 2015